Infrastructure

This book provides an overview and assessment of infrastructure's legal and governance underpinnings.

Infrastructure is often thought of as a term referring only to the physical entities – pipes, cables, utility poles, highways, airports – that facilitate the transmission of water, gas, telecommunications, and electricity, as well as enabling both private and public transportation, and serving to house more or less public services such as health care and schools. However, infrastructure planning and implementation are not reducible to bricks and mortar. The complex process requires drawing from and sometimes re-inventing or recycling legal tools, from construction contracts to financing 'deals', which are often taken for granted by both practitioners and urban studies scholars. These are as important today as they were when the first railway lines were built, and to a large extent they remain just as invisible: the avalanche of drawings and photographs of planned or in-process fancy buildings tends to hide from view the behind-the-scenes negotiations and decision-making that had to happen before construction could start and which in some cases continue afterwards. This book does not ignore the material and nonhuman aspects of infrastructure. But, focusing on the legal and governance underpinnings of infrastructure projects, via a series of key terms that refer to hybrid legal processes, the book offers an important socio-legal supplement to the current 'infrastructure turn'.

This book will be of interest to students in the areas of socio-legal studies, urban sociology, urban studies, urban geography, planning, public law, and contract law, as well as practitioners involved in infrastructure projects.

Mariana Valverde is Professor Emeritus at the Centre for Criminology and Sociolegal Studies at the University of Toronto, Canada.

Part of the NEW TRAJECTORIES IN LAW
Series Editors
Adam Gearey, *Birkbeck College, University of London*
Prabha Kotiswaran, *Kings College London*
Colin Perrin, *Commissioning Editor, Routledge*
Mariana Valverde, *University of Toronto*

For information about the series and details of previous and forthcoming titles, see www.routledge.com/New-Trajectories-in-Law/book-series/NTL.

A GlassHouse Book

Infrastructure

New Trajectories in Law

Mariana Valverde

Routledge
Taylor & Francis Group
a GlassHouse Book

First published 2022
by Routledge
4 Park Square, Milton Park, Abingdon, Oxon OX14 4RN

and by Routledge
605 Third Avenue, New York, NY 10158

This is a GlassHouse book

Routledge is an imprint of the Taylor & Francis Group, an informa business

British Library Cataloguing-in-Publication Data
A catalogue record for this book is available from the British Library

Library of Congress Cataloging-in-Publication Data
A catalog record has been requested for this book

ISBN: 978-1-032-18526-2 (hbk)
ISBN: 978-1-003-25498-0 (pbk)
ISBN: 978-1-003-25497-3 (ebk)

DOI: 10.4324/9781003254973

Typeset in Bembo
by Apex CoVantage, LLC

Contents

Introduction   1

1 Audit   15

2 Bonds   28

3 Community consultations   36

4 Credit ratings   45

5 'The deal'   54

6 High-speed rail   63

7 Public-private partnerships   78

8 Smart cities   90

9 'Value for money' assessments   104

10 Conclusion   113

    Index   120

Introduction

Foucault began his famous inquiry into 'sexuality' as the truth of the modern self by asking what came before, and he commenced his inquiry into madness and medicine by asking what came before modern 'insanity'. So too, this book begins by noting that the term 'infrastructure' has over a few short years come to occupy the semantic, the material, and the political space(s) previously occupied by 'public works'.

But the ubiquitous term 'infrastructure' does more than occupy the space previously allocated, in pre-neoliberal times of easy state spending and grand planning, to 'public works'. What is most remarkable about its usage is that the term is used by politicians to justify government spending, even in times/places of austerity. Only the tattered remnants of old Labour would today promote 'public works'. But 'infrastructure' is seen as an unalloyed good. Even tax-cutting politicians such as former US president Donald Trump claim to be in favour of infrastructure, always described as a state "investment" – as if that were not the same as a public expenditure – even though in the US privately owned, profitable toll highways or bridges are scarce. Trump did not implement an infrastructure programme, but he repeatedly announced "infrastructure week" without his supporters being forced to learn the hard lesson that new infrastructure usually requires new taxes.

Semantic shifts are revealing. Whereas the term 'public works' calls to mind a state that has sufficient capacity to carry out major works, and/or to support subnational governments such as municipalities in their projects, the term 'infrastructure' has come to connote and indeed even denote 'public-private partnerships' (PPPs). As shown in detail in Chapter 7, 'PPP' is one of those highly ideological and vague terms – like 'democracy' or 'the rule of law' – that appear to refer to something specific but are so vague that much space is provided for authorities of various sorts including private ones to carry out all manner of diverse activities.

DOI: 10.4324/9781003254973-1

The slippage from 'infrastructure' to 'PPPs' has been facilitated, or arguably created, by the political and cultural climate within which these terms arose, a climate in which any infrastructure project beyond local road paving is deemed to be automatically a candidate for a PPP. In the global North, governments of both liberal–centrist and right-wing neoliberal orientations promote this view, often implicitly through their procurement practices rather than overtly in public discourse. In the global South, global corporations and financing entities (the World Bank in particular) actively confuse infrastructure with PPPs, as seen in this snippet of the World Bank's official advice:

> Building modern, sustainable, and reliable infrastructure is critical for meeting the rising aspirations of billions of people around the globe. Infrastructure investment helps raise economic growth rates, offers new economic opportunities, and facilitates investment in human capital. PPPs can be a tool to deliver much needed infrastructure services.[1]

This claim, which is worded in a misleadingly neutral manner – the World Bank has no advice to emerging economies on infrastructure financing methods other than PPPs – is clearly grounded in larger cultural and political trends: the macro-factors that often go under the label 'neoliberalism' (although in the interests of clarity and concreteness, I will largely avoid using this overused term.)

The notion that the public sector is inherently overly bureaucratic and inefficient and is well advised to enter into 'partnerships' with the private sector if major projects are going to be carried out 'on time and on budget', a notion that while not explicitly articulated by the World Bank (whose texts are always careful to not disrespect state sovereignty) is foundational for what I call 'the infrastructure-enabling field'[2], is rooted in the larger-scale decline of the ideals of the post-World War II welfare state.[3] PPPs, also known as P3s, while not being used to further

---

1 This paragraph is on the front page of the World Bank's primer for global South countries at www.worldbank.org/en/topic/publicprivatepartnerships.

2 The notion of 'field' deployed here is partly borrowed from Pierre Bourdieu's famous analysis – although in keeping with today's 'assemblage' thinking, I would de-emphasize connections among people and put more stress on institutional habits and relations, as well as on the materiality of particular infrastructures.

3 Within urban studies, there is a vast literature on 'neoliberal urbanism', with Jamie Peck being perhaps the most influential author in English. More explicitly focused on infrastructure under neoliberal conditions are diverse sources, such as Deb Cowen's influential

neoliberal aims in every instance – since creativity in governance is always possible and there are progressive instances of PPPs – are nevertheless connected, as a governance trend, to explicitly neoliberal political and social views.

These neoliberal views – here examined only as they become visible in the infrastructure space – stand in sharp contrast to the 'big state' ambitions of proto-welfare state programmes such as the American New Deal of the 1930s, which famously utilized the powers of the US federal government to create major infrastructure projects – a remarkable achievement in a country in which infrastructure had historically been the responsibility of municipal and state governments. So 'public works' is or was closely linked to the rise of the 'welfare state', in the global North at any rate, from the water and sewerage projects of London's Metropolitan Board of Works to President Franklin D. Roosevelt's (FDR) Depression-era New Deal. Tellingly (as Raymond Williams might have noted if he were still among the living), the term 'infrastructure' began to literally replace the term 'public works' towards the end of the twentieth century – at a time when not coincidentally top-down, state-initiated projects were coming under great suspicion among both right-wing and left-wing thinkers and actors.[4]

However, in addition to the affinities between trends in views of the state and ways of naming state projects in areas such as utilities and transportation, there is also an important historical and philological link between 'infrastructure' and 'PPP' that is not well-known. In the 1870s, the term 'infrastructure' began to be used by French engineers to refer to the preparatory work that public bodies (municipalities

---

book *The deadly life of logistics* (Minneapolis, MN, University of Minnesota Press, 2014). A book that can in retrospect be seen as foundational for what could be called sociolegal studies of infrastructure is Stephen Graham and Simon Marvin, *Splintering urbanisms: networked infrastructures, technology mobilities and the urban condition* (New York, Routledge, 2001). An influential work that does not put itself forward as a study of infrastructure but arguably is, Timothy Mitchell's *Carbon democracy: political power in the age of oil* (London, Verso, 2011). Recently, global South scholars influenced by postcolonial insights have drawn attention to the Eurocentric bias of much infrastructure discourse and practice, with implications for poorer parts of the global North. Ananya Roy and Colin MacFarlane are two leading scholars in this important field; see inter alia Colin McFarlane, "The politics of urban sanitation" in Charlotte Lemanski, ed., *Citizenship and infrastructure: practices and identifies of citizens and the state* (London, Routledge, 2019), 43–63.

4 In earlier work, I have shown that the suspicion of 'big government' and large-scale planning that began in the 1970s is rooted not only in right-wing neoliberal views but also in the rejection of grand planning amongst planners and civic activists that can be dated to the 1960s work of Jane Jacobs. See Mariana Valverde, *Everyday law on the street: city governance in an age of diversity* (Chicago, IL, University of Chicago Press, 2012), Chapter 8.

and/or states) would do to facilitate railway building – then a purely private enterprise. Such preparatory work implicitly assigned to the state included legal manoeuvres, especially expropriation and proto-planning regulations, but often also financial backing. However, the state's role was not confined to using its legal authority (e.g. the compulsory purchase or expropriation of private land) and its fiscal and borrowing powers; the preparatory 'infra' work that either through explicit agreements or by convention was ascribed to the state also included and referred to the physical preparation of the land (e.g. carrying out earthworks to flatten the terrain). Similarly, the work done by private corporations was not limited to construction but also required complex legal and financial moves, many of them innovative.

Thus, in its original version, infrastructure was not an endeavour neatly divided between a public realm invested with the legal powers of the state vs. a private sector with economic might and financial objectives. Both 'sides', if one can even see them as sides, were/are composed of and constantly generating what actor-network scholars call 'hybrid' assemblages,[5] in which material, legal, cultural, and financial dimensions interact, often in unique, site-specific relationships, where the term 'site-specific' includes legal peculiarities.[6]

The historical origins of the word 'infrastructure' thus corroborate contemporary research findings to the effect that PPPs are currently integral to infrastructure thinking and planning at most relevant scales (though some governments, especially at the local level, reject the PPP model and continue to use traditional financing and procurement practices). While in the last decades of the twentieth century lively debates about the merits of public vs private infrastructure financing and decision-making raged, in the scholarly literature as well as in

---

5 The de facto existence of PPPs in the nineteenth century has been well documented in the US – David C. Perry, ed., *Building the public city: the politics, governance and finance of public infrastructure* (London, SAGE, 1995).

6 I have called attention to the site-specific and jurisdiction-specific character of most infrastructure projects, across historical periods, in a book chapter: Mariana Valverde, "Ad hoc governance: public authorities and North American local infrastructure in historical perspective" in Michelle Brady and Randy Lippert, eds., *Neoliberal governmentalities and ethnography* (Toronto, University of Toronto Press, 2016), 199–219. The technical literature on infrastructure pays attention to material peculiarities such as flood risks, but the legal peculiarities of different projects often go unstudied. The legal peculiarities of one specific project (never realized) are detailed in Alexandra Flynn and Mariana Valverde, "Where the sidewalk ends: The governance of Waterfront Toronto's Sidewalk Labs deal" *Windsor Yearbook of Access to Justice*, vol. 36, 2019, 263–83.

public discourse, today, the prevalence of PPPs, indeed their taken-for-grantedness in many contexts, is well established (even though as Chapter 7 will show there is no one accepted definition of a PPP). But in addition to noting the growing acceptance of PPPs, a useful way to begin this book is to note that the contingent historical origins of the term "infrastructure" help to inscribe a particular theory of the respective roles of the state vs. private enterprise in the heart of the ever-evolving assemblages of financing mechanisms, contracts, architects' drawings, construction methods, representational practices, labour practices and earth-moving practices that the capacious banner of 'infrastructure' enables. It is not coincidental that the word was first used in English in the 1880s, as a direct borrowing from French, but then remained little used until the neoliberal revolution. The historical weight, if one can call it that, of the term suggests, perhaps subliminally, that the state is meant to use its peculiar powers (expropriation, planning law exemptions, business tax reductions) to facilitate privately built infrastructure projects, even when the resulting physical assets are privately operated and even privately owned. That there is an implicit theory at the heart of the very term 'infrastructure' becomes evident when paying attention both to the history of the term and its current usage.

Legal and socio-legal literature

There is a very large 'technical' literature on infrastructure by engineers and experts in topics such as railways, water and sewage systems, and so on. This literature tends to either ignore legal and governance factors or take them for granted, as if they were immovable objects. In other venues, one finds an interesting literature from the social sciences, mainly urban studies and anthropology, representing what is often called 'the infrastructure turn'. This includes many fascinating studies of how people actually use infrastructures, perhaps against the grain (especially in the global South, where such 'guerrilla' tactics as illegally tapping into electricity lines are common). Anthropological studies shed much light on which infrastructure needs rise to the top of the political agenda and which do not, and they help to provincialize Eurocentric/global North biases inherent in the ideal of large, connected networks of smoothly functioning, expensive, and expansive systems. A recent collection, whose main geographic focus is Africa, representing this trend is *Citizenship and Infrastructure*. A very influential earlier collection that can in retrospect be seen as key in the critical infrastructure studies field is Stephen Graham and Simon

Marvin's 2001 *Splintering Urbanism*, which draws attention to the way in which the provision of certain infrastructures in certain places can aggravate inequality, as 'premium spaces' are made in some places that make the rest of the city look more drab or dysfunctional than before.[7]

Amongst legal scholars, administrative and other public lawyers concerned with transparency and accountability or lack thereof in PPPs have done a great deal to encourage critical questioning of governance tools largely taken for granted amongst practitioners and among the politicians who commission works. We will now take a brief look at some of this scholarship, which, to simplify, can be summarized in Ellen Dannin's article titled "Crumbling Infrastructure, Crumbling Democracy".[8]

Legal scholarship has not played much of a role in the so-called infrastructure turn, but there are studies whose insights could be used by social scientists and urban planners working on infrastructure governance (especially if published in venues other than law reviews, which are hardly read outside of law schools). A key area of legal scholarship is administrative law. Ellen Dannin's article just cited is a great example of how administrative law insights about accountability could help avoid some of the 'bad practices' that one finds in infrastructure procurement transnationally. Other administrative law scholars have contributed their analyses, such as Gerald Hodge in Australia, whose extensive international publication record draws attention to the way in which current infrastructure financing and procurement practices underplay or even ignore the public interest in part by the taken-for-granted use of private law tools, mainly contracts, instead of public law tools such as planning laws.[9]

We will provide a note on the dearth of socio-legal studies of infrastructure governance as a postscript to the section on legal literatures.

---

7 Stephen Graham and Simon Marvin, *Splintering urbanism: networked infrastructures, technological mobilities and the urban condition* (London, Routledge, 2001). This type of sociopolitical analysis of infrastructures is now being developed in global South contexts in innovative ways; see, for example, Charlotte Lemanski, ed., *Citizenship and infrastructure: practices and identities of citizens and the state* (London, Routledge, 2019).

8 Ellen Dannin, "Crumbling infrastructure, crumbling democracy: infrastructure privatization contracts and their effects on state and local governments" *Northwestern Journal of Law and Social Policy*, vol. 6, no. 1, 2011, 47–105.

9 Gerald Hodge, "Public private partnerships and legitimacy" *University of New South Wales Law Journal*, vol. 29, no. 3, 2006, 318–27, and many subsequent publications. For the US, see Jody Freeman's overview, "The contracting state" *Florida State University Law Review*, 2000, 155–239, and within US planning law, Lynn Sagalyn, "Public-private development" *Journal of the American Planning Association*, vol. 73, no. 1, 2007, 1–18.

As mentioned previously, administrative law scholars have noted, often with alarm, the growing importance of private law tools, especially contracts, in infrastructure planning and procurement – writing about the risks of 'planning by contract' and, generally, 'the contracting state'. The warnings issued for decades now by administrative law scholars guarding the public interest and democratic accountability processes could have been followed by socio-legal scholars' empirical studies of infrastructure planning and implementation – but that has not been the case, unfortunately.

One interesting example of a major socio-legal study that could have been presented as an empirical follow-up to public lawyers' warnings about the 'contracting state', but was in fact presented as a contribution to international law, specifically the literature on transnational conflicts over water and river basins, is an Australian collective study of two hydroelectric dam projects in the Mekong River.[10] The Mekong is certainly an important global example of a river basin that is transnational, with four of the six riparian states being included in the multifaceted Australian study. And yet, aiming the book at an audience interested in international law and perhaps environmental law does a disservice to the deep research done for the book, which revealed many interesting details about topics central to infrastructure governance, such as state credit ratings and the role of financing in determining the ultimate shape and success of different plans.

There are many studies that greatly add to our collective knowledge of the legal and governance underpinnings of infrastructure planning and delivery, but most often these are written under the auspices of a field other than socio-legal studies – urban planning, environmental assessments, logistics, financialization, etc. In sum, there are numerous *de facto* studies of the socio-legal 'infrastructure' of infrastructure, but they do not present themselves as such, for the most part. Looking on the bright side, however, future scholarship may change this, since the subfield of the anthropology of infrastructure appears to be flourishing, especially in global South contexts, and socio-legal scholars are today keenly aware of the importance of empirical studies (often by anthropologists) of the way in which infrastructure planning and delivery, as well as infrastructure absences and failures, are experienced by ordinary people.

---

10 Ben Boer, Philip Hirsch, Fleur Johns, Ben Saul, and Natalia Scurrah, *The Mekong: a socio-legal approach to river basin development* (London, Routledge/Earthscan, 2016).

Beyond 'privatization'

Legal scholars' concern to preserve the ideals of public law in democratic societies is often reflected in political debates about 'privatization', debates in which left-wing parties and labour unions play a more
prominent role than scholars. Much attention has been paid, since the
Thatcher 'revolution', to the negative consequences of the outright privatization of formerly public assets (hospitals, toll highways, public housing, prisons, schools). Unfortunately, many participants in these debates
often confuse readers about what is and is not becoming private. In the
case of housing, whether a residence is owned by the local government
or by the resident (perhaps a former tenant, perhaps a capitalist) is certainly the key variable: but this is not the case for infrastructure generally. In regard to many types of infrastructure, the ownership of an asset
(say an electricity plant) is not the only important variable. Electricity
production, for example, can be or could be in private hands while electricity prices are highly regulated. Hence it is important to distinguish
between private ownership and private-sector control of infrastructure
provision and pricing (as we see in the current debate on regulating Big
Tech since few are proposing nationalizing Internet access).

One aim of this book is to help readers avoid instantly taking sides
in abstract debates (is privatization good or bad?) Instead, this book
will show that the public interest can be furthered even in the absence
of wholesale nationalization (or municipalization). And vice versa.
Even when the final physical asset is owned by the government (as
is the case in almost all of Canada, in US municipalities, and some
northern European countries for infrastructures other than fibre-optic
networks), the process by which infrastructure is planned, financed,
and built can be pretty much the same as that used in the case of private ownership of the eventual 'asset'. **Public ownership** of a service
or a network can and often now does coexist with private profits and
private-sector control.

In some jurisdictions, such as the UK, one now sees rising political
resistance to what is rather loosely called privatization. In my view, it
is useful to reserve the latter term for either substituting private-sector
employees for civil servants and/or selling public assets to the private
sector. Notably, outsourcing does not equal privatization, if the key issue
is control and accountability. For instance, a publicly built service such
as a hospital may continue to employ members of the traditional public-
sector unions of nurses and orderlies, but may at the same time struc-
turally rely upon PPPs that touch upon employment relations without

a wholesale replacement of unionized by non-unionized personnel. The hospital could further engage in some novel 'privatization', such as charging patients for services that used to be provided gratis, and such a 'privatization' might not incur the ire of public-sector unions. Similarly, when public-sector workers are replaced by employees of private firms, a common situation, that does not automatically mean that the government service is wholly privatized. In Canada, for instance, much work previously done by Post Office employees is now done by the private sector since in many cases the local Post Office has been closed and the work has been contracted out to major drugstore chains. And yet Canada Post remains a public agency – one that like many other public agencies is expected to become increasingly 'entrepreneurial' and business-like, but it would be misleading to say that it has been wholly privatized.

Hence, to help citizens and public-sector lawyers better understand the many questions that need to be asked of public authorities sponsoring infrastructure projects today – the main goal of this book – reviving the by now tired 'public-sector vs. private-sector' debate, as if there were two mutually exclusive static and closed spheres, would be most unhelpful. Each service and each major common asset is its own hybrid network, to use the currently popular language of actor-network theory, and requires careful analysis of the many relationships that constitute it, legally and in practice. The focus of this book, therefore, will not be on 'privatization' – an abstract term that is often sloppily used – but rather on specific mechanisms – financial, legal, cultural, political – found throughout what I will call 'the infrastructure-enabling field'.

The infrastructure-enabling field – currently replete with consultants, accountants, and corporate lawyers, as well as the traditional bankers, engineers, and politicians who had more exclusive power over public works in the past – is dominated by 'global' firms based in advanced capitalist countries. However, one must be as careful about loose uses of the term 'globalization' as about the sloppy uses of 'privatization'. The predominance of a handful of 'global' firms headquartered in major global North cities does not mean that the governance architecture of infrastructure projects in the global North is being faithfully replicated around the world. In any case, there is no such thing as a paradigm instance of infrastructure in the global North. Governing habits and traditions that are often quite localized persist and can trump the latest neoliberal management trends, and, further, actors everywhere demonstrate creativity as they put together 'deals' in their own context. Certainly, there are some valid generalizations: the most important one is probably that in the global South, the World Bank and the International

Monetary Fund (IMF) play a far larger role in pushing for particular infrastructure governance frameworks than in the global North. However, an introductory account such as this book can emphasize commonalities in logics, norms, and techniques across geographical and socio-economic divides. Each infrastructure project has social, economic, political, financial, and environmental peculiarities, which need to be understood by engaged citizens as well as policymakers.[11] But as an overview of the world of infrastructure planning, this book will emphasize organizational habits, taken-for-granted assumptions, and techniques of governance that are quite widely distributed across the world. The aim here is to provide citizens, researchers, and policymakers with some helpful initial insights, but they will still need to undertake their own studies of specific projects, asking their own questions.

Representing infrastructure: a cultural studies note

Historian of science Ian Hacking drew attention long ago to the impact of the 'avalanches of printed numbers' that modernizing nineteenth-century states produced (censuses, factory inspectors' reports, mortality tables, etc.) His early work on what some including the present author call 'knowledge formats' remains influential today. And indeed, in the infrastructure-enabling field there are avalanches of printed numbers, produced by computer-aided engineers as well as financial 'quants', but these are not usually shown to the public. What predominates in official discourse on infrastructure – as demonstrated in Chapter 6 – are not financial figures, or indeed numbers of any type, but rather avalanches of literally glowing drawings and photographs of planned or in-process structures. Both governments and private companies regularly post full-colour images on their websites before, during, and after actual infrastructure projects, and citizens are interpellated as viewers of professionally made images more than as readers of charts or texts. For the most part, the pictures feature imaginary rosy futures rather than actual landscapes or photographs of existing buildings. Those pictures of the rosy future are usually drawings generated by landscape

---

11 A certain largely Marxist approach to research on these issues (David Harvey being a leading name here) tends to assume that if transnational finance can be shown to be involved in or driving certain processes, the result can only be harmful to local communities, especially marginal groups within them. That is often true, but in my view, the effects need to be documented; they cannot be deduced in advance.

architects. On their part, the photographs routinely included in press releases feature either highly staged ribbon cuttings, where politicians awkwardly pose in construction helmets, or else unusually large construction equipment of the type that impresses passing toddlers. The marketing images appear to be – like all visuals – true representations of reality. As pictures, they supposedly allow citizens to 'see with their own eyes' how their taxes are being spent and how both big government and big construction companies are moving society forward.[12]

But the avalanches of pretty pictures reveal nothing about the behind-the-scenes negotiations that had to happen before construction could start (and which in many cases continue afterward, as decisions and budgets are revisited along the way, though the relevant pretty pictures produced at the early approval stage are seldom revised). Citizens ought to beware of pretty pictures.

Conclusion

Buildings, trains, wires, and pipes are certainly important, indeed crucial for life today, and not only in cities. This book does not ignore the material and nonhuman aspects of infrastructure. But since this is a socio-legal book, it focuses mainly on the legal and governance underpinnings of large infrastructure projects. Focusing on the infrastructure-enabling field is much needed because the existing literature consists largely of case studies, usually illuminating but highly limited in time and space. The case-study format tends to hide from view key mechanisms, terms, legal tools, and practices of inscription that are commonly used across jurisdictions and across types of projects, and that as mentioned above cross the divide between publicly owned or operated and privately owned and/or operated projects.

The literature on infrastructure and logistics (largely located within urban studies, urban planning, and, in the case of global South projects, development studies) tends to either ignore the legal and governance underpinnings or else it focuses only on particularly egregious practices –

---

12 Two infrastructure websites I have closely examined recently are those of Metrolinx, the transit agency in the Greater Toronto Area, and HS2, the British high-speed train project, but over the years, I have seen mountains of reports and have visited countless infrastructure-related websites. Unfortunately for democracy, all manner of media, including social media, as well as mass media, reproduce the pretty pictures as they are and rely on official press releases for the accompanying text, instead of seeking to provide more objective accounts.

'boondoggles'. In the case of the global North scandals, 'white elephant' projects are generally discussed as unusual instances of malfeasance or stupidity; in the case of the global South, by contrast, case studies usually resort to a generalized suspicion of government corruption. The World Bank has been a major producer and disseminator of norms and techniques widely utilized across the whole infrastructure-enabling field, even projects with no World Bank involvement. It is certainly not coincidental that the World Bank has in recent years created a new agency called the **Public–Private Infrastructure Advisory Authority**, aimed primarily at African countries but extending its supervisory gaze into middle-income countries in other regions, notably Colombia.

The focus on the spectre of corruption which is shared by journalists and by global agencies generates, intentionally or not, a highly normative agenda, one that contains and relies upon a distinct racialization of potential offenders vs. potential truth-tellers and saviours. However, the agenda of this book is descriptive and analytical, not normative (that being perhaps the key difference between standard legal analysis and socio-legal analysis). Events and behaviours that might under some circumstances be labelled as 'corruption' certainly play a key role in the approval processes and in the outcomes of particular projects. But scrutinizing either instances of outright corruption – or, more interestingly, the governance carried out under the banner of anti-corruption by UN-affiliated bodies, global banks, consultant firms, non-government bodies such as Transparency International, and development agencies from the global North – would not tell us anything about infrastructure as a field.

Putting to one side the old and inherently normative category of corruption – something that would in turn bracket the virtue universally prescribed as a cure for corruption, transparency – will facilitate a close examination of the tools, inscription practices, discursive habits, and governing and finance practices that are common to both corrupt and noncorrupt projects and that constitute the infrastructure-enabling field.

The book's rationale and organization

One could write a good introductory text on the governance mechanisms used in the infrastructure field as a series of well-chosen case studies. However, the vast majority of the case studies I have personally carried out are in the province of Ontario and so by definition are not representative. And relying on secondary sources for other case studies would be risky: each published study of a distant jurisdiction cannot provide all the context necessary to understand the significance of the project's governance architecture. Because of that, and also in order to fill a need unmet by case studies – namely, general reflections on the practices that have come to dominate the field around the world – I have chosen a different format. Proceeding alphabetically – to emphasize that the present book is not a systematic study but a somewhat idiosyncratic collection of reflections – I go over a set of what one can call either 'assemblages' or 'governing practices', depending on one's favourite theory framework.

The words that give the chapters their titles are not wholly arbitrary, however. On the one hand, they are all familiar. And yet the words, alone or in routinized combinations, have acquired a certain air of specialization and expertise (e.g. 'smart cities'). Some of the chapter titles are terms that developed in financial circles (audits, bonds, credit ratings), but they are chosen because they are no longer confined to the financial world. They are more than technical and have gone into common usage – as keywords of our time, perhaps.

Terms that have become trendy or even overused can yield results if closely scrutinized. That is the case with Chapter 5, on 'the art of the deal'. This is a phrase notoriously associated with Donald Trump's view of business, but it can be turned into an analytical lens to examine the important and usually hidden effects of the scale (as geographers say) at which infrastructure is planned and built, which is almost always, today, that of the single 'deal'. To return to the introduction to this chapter: the era of 'public works' favoured national networks (British Rail; the Eisenhower network of highways), but in the age of infrastructure the default setting is the single 'deal'. The chapter focusing on the current British high-speed train project (HS2) is among other things an analysis of the consequences of pushing infrastructure needs onto the Procrustean bed of the 'deal'.[13]

Finally, while the book stays away from grand political declarations about what "we" "must" do – I am part of a generation effectively vaccinated against preachiness by the ubiquitous socialist rhetoric of the 1970s – a clear political agenda is promoted here: that of effective democracy, especially at the local level. The brief chapter on how 'community consultations' proceed focuses on the decline of effective

---

13 Elsewhere, I have argued that universities, which in many instances have become important urban developers, also tend to see, to plan, and to finance infrastructure (new buildings, usually) at the scale of the single deal, instead of having a long-term, evidence-based campus plan. See Mariana Valverde et al., "Public universities as real estate developers in the age of 'the art of the deal'" *Studies in Political Economy* Vol. 101, 1, 2020, 35–58.

democracy, but all other chapters also contribute to what I hope will be a greater understanding of how it is that large amounts of public money are being poured into projects that citizens had no say in choosing and very little input in how they are implemented.

This introduction was written in the summer of 2021, as President Biden and the US House of Representatives announced a hugely expensive 'infrastructure package', while European Union (EU) member states debated how to spend hundreds of millions of euros of COVID recovery funds. These events make this book timely because it aims to encourage citizens to formulate the right questions, especially in regard to legal tools and financing practices, in relation to their local infrastructure plans and projects.

Chapter 1

Audit

An influential professor of accounting at the London School of Economics (LSE), Michael Power, has for over two decades now drawn attention to the ways in which the techniques and the broader logic of 'auditing', for a long time confined to checking flows of money with the aim of ensuring corporate expenditures were properly authorized, have spread like wildfire to all manner of non-financial fields. In his 1997 book *The Audit Society: Rituals of Verification*, he describes the adoption of the language of 'audit', together with some of audit's techniques, in areas and entities where quantification, never mind monetization, is either impossible or counterproductive.

The travels of audit talk and audit methods beyond the original function of an audit (meant to reassure board members that the managers of the entity of which they are directors are conducting themselves honestly) are in large part due to the fact that the work of many institutions has recently become subject to greater scrutiny by government funders, by international bodies both official and not (e.g. non-governmental organizations (NGOs)), and/or by wary consumers. It would be possible now to collect information about the working of audits and audit-like techniques in fields as diverse as international aid, the state regulation of charities, and the experiences of hospital patients.

As Power and others after him have shown, we now have audits of medical practice geared to patient satisfaction; we have 'safety audits' of institutional or public spaces (often carried out after pressure from women's groups); we have audits of the quality of education at post-secondary institutions; there are 'supply-chain audits' of transnational corporations prompted by consumer or labour groups, designed to denounce and root out exploitative labour conditions or environmental harms, or both; and so on.

Power notes that whatever the particular target of this or that 'audit', most audits function as 'quality labels'. In many cases, the quality in

DOI: 10.4324/9781003254973-2

question is not as easy to define as that ensured by the older label "made with union labour". One reason why the process of being certified or authorized in these fields is not as easy to determine as whether a labour union exists in a plant is that the idea of quality assurance or audit only emerges after the fact once a space or business or activity has been functioning for some time. That is the case with the 'safety audits' that women's groups have imposed on many education and housing providers. When an audit concerning some risk that was not within the original plan is instituted after the fact, the audit has to use measuring sticks that had not been anticipated ex ante – in the case of a campus, when the parking lot or the building in question were built or designed. That means that obtaining the data necessary for the *ex post* audit is much more difficult than the task faced by accountants auditing financial statements in firms long used to having their financials audited. Corporate staff members are trained to be careful about figures being filled in and authorizing signatures being obtained during the course of the fiscal year, well in advance. In situations such as the campus safety audit, however, the lack of fit between the initial, traditional purpose of the entity in question and the information that is later required creates problems (as Marilyn Strathern and many others have shown in the context of the audits of the quality of British academic research and education[1]).

It is nevertheless the case that when a new type of audit or evaluation is created/imposed, that action will have recursive effects on the organization and on personnel. Wendy Espeland's justly famous study of the recursive effects of US law school ranking systems shows that once the indicators used to generate rankings are known to the institution managers, all manner of creative moves will be made in order not so much to game the system as to use it to one's advantage.[2]

---

1 Marilyn Strathern, "The tyranny of transparency" *British Educational Research Journal*, vol. 26, no. 3, 2000, 309–21. The large literature on academic audits is largely British, with some Australian contributions, probably due to the central government's increasing control over universities in those countries, which has facilitated the imposition of standardized audits and similar measures. Canada and the US have far more decentralized university systems, which likely explains why quality assurance and audit-like mechanisms play a smaller role.

2 Michael Sauder and Wendy Espeland, "The discipline of rankings: tight couplings and organizational change" *American Sociological Review*, vol. 74, no. 1, 2009, 63–82. The study found, among other things, that second-tier law schools began to reject well qualified Black applicants deemed likely to choose first-tier schools so as not to negatively impact the indicator 'proportion of acceptance offers accepted'.

In the world of infrastructure, there are of course inspection and quality assurance mechanisms that focus on the bricks and mortar. However, there is a growing emphasis on mechanisms to ensure 'good governance' (a vague notion currently institutionalized in the financial world's focus on 'environmental, social, and governance' (ESG) factors). In regard to the quest for measures of the vague idea of good governance, a number of techniques have been devised, including the ubiquitous 'value for money' calculations meant to justify procurement models (see Chapter 9).

Interestingly, however, UN bodies and international lenders constantly deplore the poor quality of data needed to do proper assessments or audits of infrastructure projects. Indeed, given that most large infrastructure projects are not subject to after-the-fact independent evaluation,[3] there are likely professional associations that certify the quality of welding, but it is unclear how any audit-like process could gather the information necessary to render a trustworthy judgement of the quality of governance. Why then insist on audits and transparency mechanisms? It is possible that the reason for the unceasing demand for data that are not regularly collected or that do not serve the institution's own purposes is the structural fact that demanding audits plays a very useful role for the entities that require or expect audits. The request for certain data that might facilitate some kind of external audit but is not regularly collected by the entity in question serves to download responsibility for many problems (including lack of data) onto the institutions being audited. The institution or department can easily be chastised for not having collected the right data or for not presenting data in the right form – criticisms that absolve the higher-level entity seeking to impose audits (usually a government or a transnational body such as the World Bank) from responsibility. The hand-wringing about 'lack of data' regularly performed across the entire field of sponsors of audits may or may not help to generate good data, but it will certainly help to popularize the notion that all institutions but especially those in receipt of public funds have to make themselves not only visible but accountable, in quantitative terms, to governments and to the public.

As institutions are pushed to make themselves auditable, improving the organization's score in relation to the newer, often consumer-focused goals may clash with the organization's stated, traditional

---

3 As admitted by infrastructure practitioners themselves at a World Bank workshop; see World Bank, *Value-for-money analyses: practices and challenges* (Washington, DC, World Bank, 2013).

goals. This happens when a consulting firm is hired to do a 'gender equality audit' of a corporation devoted to selling commodities, not redressing gender injustice, or when experts are asked to measure the ESG performance of a multinational company whose original purpose was to increase shareholder value.

As Power and others have shown, the great popularity of 'audit' discourse and practices well outside audit's original arena (corporate financial statements) is closely linked to wider cultural trends. One such trend, clearly visible in the world of infrastructure project planning, is a growing mistrust of powerful organizations – a trend in turn closely related to the rise of the vaguely described phenomenon known as 'populism'. Only if there is mistrust is there a call for an audit or evaluation, after all. Family members do not generally demand to audit one another's financial records, but spouses going through a divorce do have to make themselves financially transparent to the other party precisely because they no longer wish to be a family. Similarly, when physicians enjoyed higher prestige and authority, such as in Dr. Spock's 1950s, hospital boards and ministries of health would not have thought of subjecting hospital departments to audits of the quality of medical treatment and measurements of the satisfaction of patients.

The rise of the 'audit' is closely linked to, and indeed is almost synonymous with, the growing demands for institutional transparency. Other phenomena linked to the apparently limitless thirst for institutional transparency are the emergence of 'access to information' and whistle-blower protection legislation in the public sector and in the private sector, as well as the rise of NGOs that succeed in appointing themselves as issuers of 'quality labels' of sustainability or 'fair trade'.

What about the world of infrastructure? In that world, the term 'audit' merges, in practice, with other equally fashionable terms: 'evaluation' and 'performance measures'. There are of course audits of disbursements by both private corporations and the public bodies that commission and ultimately finance most infrastructure. Those sometimes generate scandals about corruption or about self-serving decisions. But the term 'audit' is also used to cover all manner of evaluations that cover rather fuzzily qualitative issues such as gender equality, the ethics of the supply chain, or good labour practices.

There is much overlap between the literature on the dissemination of the audit and the larger and more diffuse literature on risk and risk management, which makes sense since auditing is a common method for managing the risks of malfeasance (or more modestly, sending a message that these risks are being managed). Financial malfeasance has admittedly never been strictly separate from other institutional risks, especially 'reputational risk'. Currently, actors in the world of high finance who are trying to position themselves as socially responsible (with former Bank of England governor Mark Carney being a leader in this regard) are proclaiming the audit society notion that seemingly non-monetary reputational risks can quickly turn into financial risks if negative non-financial audits influence many shareholders or consumers.

The growing slipperiness of the very word 'audit' further fudges the distinction between monetary malfeasance and other problem areas that were in the past outside the remit of accountants' audits (such as where a jewellery company sources its diamonds). Today, calling for an audit may function less as a sober bean-counting operation and more as a modern secular substitute for the old Christian idea that God is personally watching each human and counting up sins that are otherwise invisible. In the infrastructure world as in other fields, the risk being managed by means of audits and other 'rituals of verification' is often a hybrid of financial and non-financial factors, a hybrid that has a strong moral flavour. The audit thus plays a role that is very similar to the ubiquitous calls for 'more transparency' that enact populist mistrust and rely on the assumption that legibility equals virtue.

In the rest of this brief chapter, I will show that audits and related calls for transparency, even if heeded, do not in fact bring about the empowerment of the people or the grassroots – the 'ordinary folks' featured in populist discourses, left-wing as well as right-wing. The 'audit society' trend certainly represents an attack on the prestige of some older sets of trusted authorities, including politicians (formerly called 'statesmen', in the period when what is now infrastructure was 'public works') and some groups of expert professionals. But it is often simply assumed, not demonstrated, that more transparency and more audits, evaluations, and commissions of inquiry will empower ordinary people. There is also often an assumption that just doing audits promotes democracy, an assumption rarely followed by close attention to who exactly does the audit and how.

A key point that is not widely understood is that, if one looks at how audits and evaluations are actually done in the field of infrastructure governance, which does not seem out of line with what has been documented in other areas, one sees that the audits are not being done by or for ordinary people. They are routinely carried out by management consultants who decide what data to gather and how to sort and analyze those data. In turn, the data do not fall from the sky: data have to be produced by a set of experts (possibly the same ones who then do the audit, possibly different ones). The rise of the 'audit' both represents and effects a general shift in authority often presented, falsely, as a victory for the common man, the consumer, and the taxpayer. In reality, however, the dissemination of 'audit society' techniques and logics in the infrastructure world mainly takes authority away from traditional experts (lawyers, engineers, scientists, university lecturers) and hands it over to a shadowy mixed group populated by accountants and business-school graduates (and in many contexts, officials from ministries or state agencies who have fully adopted the values of the PPP world [see Chapter 7]).

The default scepticism about expert opinions that marks populism may well be justified. In relation to infrastructure, the public is encouraged by the press and by opposition politicians to be suspicious of the motives of political leaders who authorized ego-boosting or electorally popular projects, and this is certainly a well-founded suspicion. On its part, the public may also believe, with good reason, that the companies that build highways and bridges and finance them can't be relied upon to hold themselves accountable. Those who are more suspicious of the state than of the private sector are often on the right wing of the spectrum, while those who are suspicious of capitalists are usually on the left. But they can all agree to declare transparency a key virtue and to recommend the audit as the right technique to achieve it. The knight in shining armour that can cut through today's right-left divide is thus one whose shield is inscribed with the magic word 'transparency' – even if in real life he/she is an accountant who is duller than Clark Kent. Transnational firms such as KPMG, Deloitte, and McKinsey employ thousands of such personnel in luxury offices spread among many cities and countries.

What is important politically is that transparency, even if we grant that it could be achieved (which is doubtful), may not amount to or even foster real accountability,[4] much less democracy – as this whole book shows. An audit, or a ranking produced by collecting more or less arbitrary piles of data,[5] is unlikely to tell us whether the entity in question, be it a law school or an infrastructure project, is on balance contributing to humankind's wellbeing.

---

4 Marilyn Strathern, "The tyranny of transparency" *British Educational Research Journal*, vol. 26, no. 3, 2000, 309–21.

5 Kevin Davis, Benedict Kingsbury and Sally Engle Merry, "Indicators as a technology of global governance" *Law and Society Review*, vol. 46, no. 1, 2012, 71–104.

Apart from the problems created when audits are extended to non-monetary processes, a common problem, one that makes any audit, however carefully done, less than useful for purposes of democratic accountability, arises from the **scale** of the audit. In the world of infrastructure, the scope of audits and evaluations is almost always the single project, the 'deal'.[6] Auditing a deal could spot ordinary monetary corruption, but it cannot tell us whether the infrastructure needs of ignored communities were more deserving than the needs that were addressed by what eventually got on the blueprint.

In general, audits are meant to spot malfeasance or negligence in the carrying out of a for-profit or non-profit business. At best they do precisely that. But they cannot guarantee virtue. Especially important in relation to infrastructure, audits cannot verify a rational allocation of resources, especially if the audit or evaluation is carried out exclusively at the scale of the single project (this bridge, this new clinic, or, rather, the respective 'deals' since the actual bridge and the actual clinic can't be easily audited). A longer-term and more geographically ambitious plan would be needed if competing infrastructure (or other) needs are to be prioritized in a rational manner. Even when national 'plans' are announced (as when in summer 2021 President Joe Biden set out some ambitious infrastructure spending targets), the process by which it was decided that some billions would be allocated to broadband access and some other number of dollars allocated to fixing bridges and roads is quite obscure. Local and state authorities are usually happy to greet with joy any infrastructure funding announcement from on high, and the mass media also generally report on such announcements as 'good news', without seeking out experts who might have evidence-based objections to the plan (such as criticizing the limited amounts devoted to 'green energy'). The notion that a country might develop a mechanism for democratically elaborating, over a period of time, a set of evidence-based infrastructure priorities seems totally beyond the pale, and in this, the global North is as guilty of democratic deficit as the South.

Let us now look at two types or sites for infrastructure audits to make the argument so far concrete.

---

6 Mariana Valverde, "Ad hoc governance: public authorities and North American local infrastructure in historical perspective" in Michelle Brady and Randy Lippert, eds., *Neoliberal governmentalities and ethnography* (Toronto, ON, University of Toronto Press, 2016), 199–220. See also Chapter 5.

The World Bank's infrastructure evaluation system

Since its creation in 1948, the World Bank has not only financed but closely governed countless large infrastructure projects or sets of projects in the global South (and, in the 1990s especially, in post-communist Eastern Europe). As the international development studies literature shows, the norms it applies in making decisions and evaluating projects have greatly contributed to the worldwide spread of what many call 'neoliberal' values and practices.[7] The Washington-based World Bank has its own evaluation department, whose name has changed over the years but is now called the "Operations Evaluation Department". In 2003, a reunion was held to celebrate the 30th anniversary of the department, at which some retired top personnel chose to speak more candidly than is the norm. Of particular interest is the fact that many live questions and answers were included in the publication, along with speeches and prepared statements.

A few nuggets from the report, posted on the World Bank website under the deliberately boring name *Operations Evaluation Department: The First 30 Years*, will illustrate some of the dilemmas that plague both those who commission infrastructure project evaluations (governments or global banks, usually) and those who are tasked with preparing them.

One issue (not explicitly discussed by any of the eminent speakers, or indeed in any of the hundreds of insider documents I have seen over the years) concerns the appropriate **scale** for evaluations. In the 1970s the Bank undertook selective evaluations at two very large scales: all of the Bank's projects in a single country (Colombia being singled out in the report) and all projects of a similar nature (say, electric power projects) around the world. These two ambitious scales of evaluation were arguably well suited to generating useful 'learnings' since each project may have had contingent reasons for working or not working out (as with any $N = 1$ situation), but both of those ambitious scales were abandoned during the heyday of the 'Washington consensus'. Instead, there was a new demand that 'borrowers' (usually, global South government ministries) do their own **project** evaluations. The Bank's own evaluation staff would henceforth be limited to **auditing** the project evaluations coming in from the periphery.

---

7 A seminal text here was James Ferguson, *The anti-politics machine: development, depolitization and bureaucratic power in Lesotho* (Minneapolis, MN, University of Minnesota Press, 1994).

This major governance change was not analyzed by any of the speakers, but it was clearly connected to the growing importance of the notion (dear to the management consulting industry) that all organizations need to monitor themselves and learn to learn from their experiences. The reports generated in the borrowing countries were initially simple 'project completion reports' (an unambitious phrase familiar to academics receiving research grants.) At the World Bank, there was apparently some push toward more substantive 'project **performance audits**' that would consider not just if the work was carried out as intended – as completion reports do – but also the perhaps unanticipated impacts. But the after-the-fact audit logic was seen as problematic due to the inevitable time lag between successive trends in development aid priorities. One speaker noted that if the Bank was pushing countries to develop their export sector, it was hardly fair to later ask whether employment growth resulted from, say, financing large cattle ranches supplying the export market. Another manager admitted to the audience of colleagues and ex-colleagues that "only in recent years has much attention been given, for instance, to assessing the impact of infrastructure projects on poor **people** as opposed to poor **areas**" (p. 29, emphasis added). Imposing new criteria after the fact through the evaluation and audit process was arguably unfair, the masters of the development universe admitted. And yet, asking only whether the project was successful on its own terms would sideline the all-important question of whether the governments in question chose the right projects in the first place – a question that World Bank staff can hardly ask explicitly since they are not supposed to impose priorities on sovereign UN member states. There is thus an unsolvable dilemma: if the Bank uses its own criteria, perhaps those reflecting later wisdom, to evaluate projects, then it's interfering. But if it becomes a passive recipient of evaluations done by the same entity that asked for the financing, how can it really audit them, other than checking that the paperwork was correct and the boxes were filled?

Even more dizzying is the fact that demanding that global South governments learn to learn from experience and honestly admit mistakes is rather rich coming from an institution known for imposing particular economic and social norms, not just technical standards, everywhere its financing goes. The neoliberal discourse about organizations needing to monitor themselves and reform themselves (becoming 'learning organizations', as business schools put it) rings hollow when applied to the scale of the World Bank itself: it is not directly accountable to any elected government or any population. Reflecting on his years heading the evaluation unit, Mervyn Weiner said in 2003 that during his time "the Bank had somehow to become a self-evaluating organization" (p. 35).

'Somehow' is the operative word here. Audits are commissioned by a governing body – the board of directors, usually – and that body is the audit's primary audience since only they have the power to fire top managers. University education is audited by government entities, for example, usually on behalf of current and future students, even if institutions have to produce 'self-studies' as a condition of continued funding, just as World Bank projects have to generate their own evaluations. While the increasingly popular 'self-study' can be seen as an infolding of the audit – that is, a project that forces organizations to scrutinize themselves as if they were outsiders – a self-auditing entity is an oxymoron.

Michael Power's argument that audits and similar mechanisms do not simply act on organizations after the fact but rather create 'the auditable organization' as something distinct and new is relevant here. Equally relevant is the literature on 'indicators' and 'rankings' mentioned earlier, which shows that organizations change rapidly in response to being audited or otherwise measured. Once they know what inputs go into the auditing/ranking system, managers naturally institute changes designed to improve their rankings, even if the changes undermine the organization's primary goal.

In the World Bank, the auditing of project reports submitted by recipient countries similarly creates an international competition: countries want and need to look efficient and corruption-free. But how could the very institution that demands accountability and even project evaluations from its clientele become visible to itself; how could it turn into a 'learning organization'? One possibility would be to converse with similar bodies – but the 30th-anniversary celebration of its evaluation unit did not feature speakers from either the IMF or any of the UN-related continent-specific development banks.

One can conclude that in setting itself up as the auditor of last resort governing countries around the world through the requested project evaluations, the World Bank is setting itself up as the world sovereign. This likely explains why it eschews the usual practice of commissioning evaluations from outside consultants and instead insists on having its own evaluation unit. After all, if the World Bank is acting like a vigilant God, but over countries rather than over individual souls, there is no higher power that can hold it accountable.

The rise of the auditor-general

The auditor-general is a figure that now bears greater political weight than simply monitoring potential corruption: currently, it bears much of the weight of 'transparency' on its shoulders. This figure is not limited to officials with that title. In the US, for instance, Congress has set up not only the overarching Government Accountability Office but also offices that perform audit-type work in regard to different government departments, and these are in addition to the many Congressional committees that also have a quasi-forensic function.

The auditor-general, as a figure found around the world despite nomenclature differences, bears a striking similarity to the coroner or medical examiner – which not coincidentally is a figure that has gained visibility and prestige in recent decades (as seen in crime novels and crime TV). 'Inquests' – according to Michel Foucault, the site where the European practice of scientific inquiry was pioneered[8] – begin by focusing on an individual death, or on a single event leading to several deaths, and they then proceed backward to identify the cause of the event. But inquests are often immersed in, and often lead to, present-day demands for future-oriented systemic or organizational change. If the audit can be described as governing institutions through malfeasance, the inquest, especially if followed by coroner's jury recommendations that are taken seriously by governments, can be described as the governing of institutions through death or disaster. Like the audit, an inquest presupposes that wrongdoing and mishaps are a fact of life, but that examining what went wrong, after the fact, will lead to improvements and reforms.

The backward-looking character of both audits/evaluations and inquests is remarkable because it seems to signal a pessimism in regard to the post-World War II ideal of the preventive welfare state – the state that was supposed to provide a safety net for the elderly, the sick, and the unemployed so they/us would not fall victim to industrial capitalism's ups and downs or to the ups and downs of personal biographies. If the state and civil society are both now reduced to waiting for wrongful or avoidable deaths to happen and then discovering their causes, that is very much at odds with the wholly future-oriented Keynesian logic whereby governments and central banks take preventive measures to ensure that disasters do not actually happen.

---

8 Michel Foucault, "Truth and juridical forms" in James Faubion, ed., *Volume III of the essential works of Michel Foucault* (New York, New Press, 2000).

In the wake of COVID-19, we can expect many countries to set up commissions of inquiry, likely mega-inquests. These retrospective, quasi-forensic exercises are likely to tell us only what is already known about health spending being skewed towards treatment, not prevention, and about the weakening of publicly funded health care and social care from the 1980s onward. But the knowledge that is there now, in locations such as nurses' unions, and that was there before COVID-19 but went unheard, is not in the prestigious format of the inquiry/inquest report. It's as if the state can only examine itself forensically – that is, looking back to probe the causes of misfortunes and deaths; it's as if the ideal of using knowledge to prevent misfortunes and deaths on a systematic society-wide basis, not just in particular situations or workplaces, has lost the lustre it had around 1945.

In Canada, where I live, the figure of the auditor-general has been imbued with increasing importance in recent decades. In the 1970s, the annual auditor-general's report did not receive end-of-the-world headlines in the media, as is the case now. Further, in Ontario, the largest province, opposition politicians seem beholden to the provincial auditor-general: they wait until they see a somewhat critical report by that figure before publicly pouncing on government mismanagement, perhaps because politicians in general are mistrusted but accountants are prestigious.

The growing influence of the auditor-general may be in part a result of weak policy research capacity in political parties (with marketing and polling research now often absorbing the bulk of the resources, even in progressive parties). And many states have cut funding for policy and evaluation research within government departments. A rather extreme example of the growing neglect of solid research beyond public opinion polls was Prime Minister Stephen Harper's 2016 move to make the census non-mandatory and thus weaken its own data power, as well as undermining the prestige of the world-leading entity Statistics Canada.

Solid data for social policy analysis purposes have become difficult to find, therefore, and in many cases, data are simply not collected. Further, many organizations (perhaps most notably police forces) have managed to find ways to circumvent or completely defeat the spirit of 'access to information' legislation passed under the banner of transparency. My colleagues who study policing and correctional institutions all agree that information is much harder to obtain now than in decades past, despite the access to information laws. And in the infrastructure world, citizens, even educated citizens in wealthy cities, are simply not given the information that would be needed to check government plans. The rise of transparency as a supposedly supra-political virtue has not on the whole served a democratic function; it has instead contributed to empowering auditor-general-style figures who, unlike researchers or journalists, are able to demand that government entities produce documents and answer questions.

In this chapter, we have focused on the popularity and prestige of audits and quasi-audit exercises such as project evaluations, a phenomenon that greatly shapes infrastructure planning (in large part by substituting after-the-fact inquiries for proactive risk reduction policies). In addition to reaffirming Michael Power's initial analysis of the consequences of the dissemination of the audit as a practice of governance that contains a certain logic, we have explored problems arising from the limited scope of most audits (the single 'deal') and the insistence on forensically looking backwards to identify malfeasance, instead of working to create democratic mechanisms for deciding collectively how to prioritize conflicting infrastructure needs. That the way in which infrastructure is planned and represented and evaluated tells us a lot about the sad state of democracy is a lesson that will be reflected in later chapters.

Chapter 2

Bonds

Traditionally, a bond refers to a debt security issued by governments, often in far smaller denominations than most privately issued securities and often to finance specific endeavours, generally either wars or infrastructure projects. The small denominations available, and the marketing of this type of security to ordinary citizens make them stand out in a financial world that for the most part operates in large sums lent and borrowed by major players in relative secrecy.

We will first explain how government bonds functioned as a key resource for the British government in the nineteenth century, as well as simultaneously serving as a key mechanism ensuring the financial security of the middle and upper classes. Then we will discuss 'war bonds', probably the most significant public finance invention of the twentieth century. We will then explain the spread of the 'bond' idea to subnational entities – municipalities but also special-purpose, arms-length corporations or agencies – and finally go on to show that bonds have veered away from their original connection with financing the state itself, having gained new and unexpected roles in infrastructure financing. The very term 'bond' is now used rather ambiguously, in keeping with the blurring of the old lines dividing public from private finance.

The British 'consol'

Readers of classic English novels will know that from the 1813 publication of *Pride and Prejudice* to E. M. Forster's *Howards End* a century later, the English middle and upper classes could plan their financial future – which of course had a huge impact on marriage markets well after Jane Austen – with much more certainty than is the case today. Victorian novel aficionados will also know that one important reason for this certainty was a commonly held security seen by all as 'safe as

DOI: 10.4324/9781003254973-3

houses': the 'consol'. 'Consol' was short for 'consolidated [government] annuities'. Thomas Piketty's magnum opus *Capital in the 20th Century* notes that since in the nineteenth-century inflation was either nonexistent or very temporary, the marriage proposals that are central to classic novel plots were 'de-risked' (as current infrastructure talk would describe it) by including consol income in marriage settlements and wills.[1] On their part, ladies who were suddenly widowed, as was common then, could plan their future knowing that a set amount of 'consols' would guarantee financial stability. The rate of return on consols was not high – three percent throughout most of the relevant period, from the 1750s through World War I. But given the Victorian era's lack of inflationary dangers, well highlighted by Piketty in his famous overviews of historical shifts in wealth, the investment provided a steady income whose effective value remained almost constant.

Consols were perpetual securities. That is, people who bought them could not redeem them unless the government decided to allow it. Thus, the government could spend the money from 'consols' sales without fear of having to suddenly return the principal. That stabilizing feature contrasted favourably with the uncertainty involved in earlier methods of public finance when European governments were exposed to the vagaries of the European financial houses that specialized in lending to governments (such as the House of Rothschild). The consol system ensured financial security, especially for widowhood or old age, to countless middle-class Britons, but it also allowed governments to plan and finance the major infrastructure projects of the nineteenth century, as well as occasional wars.

The twentieth-century war bond

The US started to sell government bonds in World War I, a decision that minimized actual or potential dependence on bankers, especially

---

1 Thomas Piketty, *Capital in the twenty-first century*. Transl. A. Goldhammer (Cambridge, MA, Harvard University Press, 2014). The mid-nineteenth century was the golden age of what Piketty dubs "patrimonial capitalism", but in many countries today, the lowering or abolition of estate taxes and similar measures have meant that wealthy families can safeguard their 'patrimonial' wealth (as distinct from income) as they did in the days of Jane Austen and Balzac. The fact that offspring of wealthy families are more likely to also land high-income jobs (in the nineteenth century, they usually lived on their rents) only magnifies this process by which inequality, under capitalism, has a tendency to increase over time, unless strong fiscal measures are introduced to reduce it.

foreign bankers. The war bonds, predictably dubbed "Liberty bonds" were issued in very small denominations, as low as $25 and $50. Thus, ordinary people, for the most part excluded from financial circuits (home mortgages, a key tool to include some working-class people in financial circuits only became common in the 1920s and 1930s), were not only allowed but positively encouraged to invest in the war effort (that is, lend their hard-earned money to the government). This at a time when investments were the preserve of the rich. The low rate of return on bonds would be counterbalanced by confidence in the security of the investment (in contrast to the volatility of stock markets) and also by the high level of patriotic pride associated with Liberty Bonds. Americans were even encouraged to buy one Liberty Bond for each newborn baby. One poster typically proclaimed, "If you can't enlist, invest". In the UK and other allied countries, such as Canada, similar posters induced many working people, including women earning unprecedented salaries in the war industries, to become small-time, cautious investors.

The American war bonds were not perpetual, unlike the British consols, but often people chose not to redeem them at maturity, continuing instead to collect the annual interest (which unlike dividends from company stocks, was fixed). When the US entered World War II in 1941, American World War II bonds (also called Liberty Bonds), were bought by an astounding 85 million Americans – that is, most of the population. These bonds continued to be honoured until 2010.

More recent wars conducted by the US and the UK, notably in Iraq and Afghanistan, have not been financed by war bonds sold to ordinary people. The US government has used the very large amount of debt room that foreign lenders have allowed it to finance these endeavours, selling vast quantities of US Treasury Bonds to China and Japan, as well as to prudent institutional investors in the US itself (such as municipalities and pension funds). Some analysts predict that the cost of servicing the Iraq War debt will over the next decades grow larger than the already huge cost of the actual war (estimated to be between $800 billion and $1 trillion, a far cry from the initial budget of $8 billion cited by the George W. Bush administration).

Thus far the US government has been able to increase its debt to eye-watering levels because it has enjoyed top credit ratings and thus very low-interest rates (much lower than those that global South governments are forced to pay). This in turn is due in large part to the privileged position of the US dollar in world finance. But many analysts, including Nobel-prize economist Joseph Stieglitz, have warned about the dangers faced by a government that chooses to continue to carry and to service huge amounts of public debt[2] in a globally competitive context in which appealing to the patriotism of ordinary Americans is not as feasible a tactic to avoid repayment of the principal as it was in earlier times. At the end of 2020, 37% of the US public debt was held by foreigners, with China being the largest creditor.

Revenue bonds and other creative securities

Revenue bonds are currently used to finance some renewable energy projects and can be issued, in many jurisdictions, by private as well as public bodies. What is a revenue bond? Government bonds were traditionally 'general obligation' bonds – that is, the money raised could be spent on any needs, just like revenue from most taxes.

A point that connects with the later chapter on 'the deal' is that the revenue bond is tied to a particular project, with the investors (those who buy the bonds) being paid back with the revenue from that project. It is common for local and state governments throughout the US, for example, to finance water infrastructure through revenue bonds. With residents of an area being effectively forced to pay whatever rate is charged for running water, the future revenue stream for water systems is pretty much assured, and hence those bonds are popular in the financial marketplace.[3] Other revenue bonds, such as for new toll highways or tunnels, are less certain; in Sydney, Australia, for example, a project for a tolled tunnel under Sydney Harbour declared bankruptcy because it did not attract enough drivers.

The previously mentioned war bonds are a kind of hybrid between a general obligation bond and revenue bond since the funds were meant to be applied to a single purpose but there was no expectation that spoils from the war would be used to repay the lenders.

2 One website purports to show not only the second-by-second increase in the US public debt but also the large gap between the publicly admitted debt and what critics call the actual debt. See www.truthinaccounting.org/about/our_national_debt

3 In countries that have allowed or even encouraged private for-profit water companies – e.g. many Latin American countries – running water and sewer service is considered more necessary and hence appears as a better investment than other utilities, such as telephones, natural gas, or even electricity. The UN-initiated Economic Commission for Latin America and the Caribbean (CELAC, in Spanish) has produced a variety of reports, available online, that shed much light on the financing of local infrastructures, including utilities.

However, revenue bonds continue to be used in contexts where future revenue streams are by no means assured. A good example is a state of Texas 'tuition revenue bond' issued in 2015 to the tune of $3 billion to finance infrastructure in state colleges. The irony here is that the state could have paid for much of the infrastructure upfront. However, a revenue bond issue was necessary because, due to the persistent suspicion of public spending that has plagued the US, the constitution of the state of Texas has hard caps on state spending, and so money had to be borrowed rather than spent.

The crises in American urban infrastructure and public schooling created by the arbitrary limits on taxes and on spending implemented in part through amending state constitutions and in part through popular referenda (especially in California) are well-known. Indeed, the sad results of that great refusal of public spending are leading politicians, even many Republicans, to support US public spending on infrastructure, at least certain kinds of infrastructure. But **how** projects are financed can be as important as the total cost (as ordinary people pondering using credit vs. debit cards know). And in relation to the 'how' of financing, it is not well-known that the revenue bond is far from being a neoliberal invention: it has been a key legal-financial tool of American infrastructure for many decades.

In the late nineteenth century, US state legislatures and courts clamped down on what was widely perceived amongst the patrician elites as the unfortunate tendency of urban leaders and their largely immigrant followers to spend a lot of money on infrastructures, especially railways.[4] Municipalities – which earlier in the nineteenth century acted as what they legally were, corporations, collecting rents from real estate and fees from transportation facilities they owned and controlled, such as public docks and city-run ferries – found themselves hamstrung by state-level elites that imagined municipalities were inherently corrupt and wasteful. To a lesser extent, this logic was also applied to state governments, though usually not until decades later. This suspicion of public spending and mistrust in elected local officials was reborn in the neoliberal 1980s, as states such as Texas imposed constitutional limits on

---

4 I draw here on a large body of published work, including Jon Teaford, *The unheralded triumph: city government in America 1870–1900* (Baltimore, MD, Johns Hopkins Press, 1984); David Perry, ed., *Building the public city: the politics, governance and finance of public infrastructure* (Thousand Oaks, CA, Sage, 1995); and Sarah Elkind, "Building a better jungle: anti-urban sentiments, public works, and political reform in American cities 1880–1930" *Journal of Urban History*, vol. 24, no. 1, 1997.

public spending and/or instituted compulsory referenda for public borrowing that as we just saw led legislators to make the financially unwise decision to float a $3 billion revenue bond issue in 2015, one that tied the funds to only one type of infrastructure (college facilities) and in turn tied the repayment to only one type of revenue (tuition). And that at a time when Texas could have simply provided the $3 billion upfront if the legislature were not subject to hard spending caps.

In the US, the revenue bond was invented in the 1890s, in large part as a result of the growing need to circumvent the tight new restrictions limiting public and especially municipal borrowing. In 1953, an infrastructure lawyer wrote that "constitutional debt limitations . . . plus the desire of government bodies to avoid elections whenever possible, have been primary factors in the great expansion of that type of financing",[5] meaning the revenue bond.

The tool also became popular among the 'special district governments' or special public authorities (much the same as what would be called 'quangos' in Thatcher's Britain). These proliferated from the late nineteenth century onward, their popularity furthered both by the declining prestige of and trust in elected local officials and by the financial straitjackets imposed on the municipal corporation itself – straitjackets which did not affect arms-length bodies such as utilities commissions or special district governments since their debts were not the debts of the municipal corporation (and came to be known as 'off the books' debt).

A key actor in the rise of the special district revenue bond was the joint State of New Jersey-State of New York Authority set up in the 1920s to run and govern the Port of New York (which for much of its history saw exports to Europe, such as wheat, first moved across the country by national railways and then shifted, through the New Jersey terminals of the various private railways, onto ships docked in New York City.) Because it was created at the state level, the Port Authority was – and remains – exempt from municipal zoning and need pay no attention at all to the desires of local elected officials in either state. A massive history of the Port Authority, *Empire on the Hudson*, shows that this authority, set up to govern the port as an autonomous business (prefiguring neoliberalism, one could say) rather than as a local public good prospered because it was able to draw on the legal and financial resources of both public entities and private corporations. Despite its money-making character,

---

5 William Alfred Rose, "Developments in revenue bond financing" *University of Florida Law Review*, vol. 6, 1953, 386.

the authority fought and eventually won a lengthy battle to have its own bonds considered sufficiently public to enjoy the tax-free status that still protects US municipal bonds today and encourages their purchase.[6] After a long battle with the FDR administration, which believed the authority should pay taxes on its business operations and its salaries, the Port Authority won the battle over tax-exempt bonds at the Supreme Court. After that, urban development corporations, school boards, and other public bodies were able to join the New York Port Authority in issuing tax-free bonds. Local authorities in the area tried repeatedly to influence the Authority, for example pushing it to run commuter trains, with variable success depending on the political context. But overall, the Authority was successful in its effort to innovatively combine the advantages of being a public body with the freedom to undertake whatever projects it wanted just like a business, largely ignoring priorities set by local elected authorities. Lawyer Austin Tobin, leader of the tax-exempt bond fight against the FDR administration, who became executive director of the Port Authority in 1942, declared that he did not want the Authority to merely administrate public works but wanted it to be able to devise "a portfolio of useful projects".[7]

Conclusion

Public bodies, including national governments, have for centuries borrowed money in the hopes that later proceeds from taxation would be sufficient to repay the loans. And for a long time now, local governments have been particularly hampered in their efforts to gain the fiscal and other revenue-raising tools that they would need to properly build and operate public infrastructures. The legal, and in the US, state-constitutional constraints on municipal revenue raising have usually been imposed by bodies above municipalities – courts of appeal, state legislatures, or, in the case of Britain, the national government – although in some cases, local taxpayers, especially in the US, have also voted against funding projects.

---

6 Jameson Doig, *Empire on the Hudson: entrepreneurial vision and public power in the Port Authority of New York and New Jersey* (New York, Columbia University Press, 2001).

7 Jameson Doig, *Empire on the Hudson: the Port Authority of New York* (New York, Columbia University Press, 2001), 260. The phrase 'portfolio of projects' is remarkable in the context because it is now constantly used in infrastructure circles, though today an even more popular phrase is 'a pipeline of projects', as if infrastructure projects from bridges to hospitals were as fungible as petroleum.

In this chapter, it has been shown that while public and journalistic discussion is often focused on the amount of public debt, the qualitative aspect of the debt is very important too. The Texas tuition revenue bond mentioned earlier is a great example of the bizarre consequences of using both the judiciary and legislatures to hamstring public spending in a way that makes it very difficult to straightforwardly address citizens' everyday infrastructure needs. Municipal finance sounds like a boring and technical subject, but understanding **how** governments at all levels borrow money is arguably necessary if citizens are going to have an informed opinion on infrastructure planning.

Chapter 3

Community consultations

Introduction

From the 1960s onward, citizen groups, in the global South as well as the global North, became more visible in infrastructure planning and delivery processes. In many countries, legal structures evolved accordingly, with urban planning in particular being substantially altered in order to include ordinary citizens – though in the common-law world, where ownership of land has an exalted status, avenues for citizen input were often limited, both by law and by political habits, to those already living and especially owning property in affected areas.[1]

The rise of environmental concerns from the 1970s onward led to novel consultation mechanisms that often included examining the probable effects of planned projects on human health and wellbeing, as well as more strictly environmental issues such as impacts on vulnerable species. Today, as one would expect, the seriousness of the investigations and the extent to which input from both citizens and environmental experts is allowed to change the plans devised by government officials and private-sector actors varies a great deal, not only among countries but also among projects in the same jurisdiction. This variability means that unlike in the golden days of 'seeing like a state' top-down, large-scale projects,[2] today community consultation is

---

1 Some Latin American constitutions have made what they call 'the social function of property' a key legal principle. As far back as the Mexican Revolution of the 1910s, this idea was used to facilitate the legal handover of agricultural land to the peasants who were working it. For one empirical study of how property owners figure as the privileged citizens to be consulted by city staff in the present, in a common-law jurisdiction, see Mariana Valverde, *Everyday law on the street: city governance in an age of diversity* (Chicago, IL, University of Chicago Press, 2012).

2 The classic source on modernizing megaprojects is James Scott, *Seeing like a state* (New Haven, CT, Yale University Press, 1999).

DOI: 10.4324/9781003254973-4

not an either/or question. Virtually every proponent of infrastructure projects will claim that such consultations are a good thing and are included in the plan. Citizen engagement is also often a legal requirement and/or a requirement imposed by international aid agencies and financing sources. This latter point is important since consultations/ citizen engagement is one of the many areas where what the law of the land says is not as important as lawyers are trained to think. International development banks, for instance, impose expectations that have as much or more persuasive power than national legal rules (since the national legal rules can often be circumvented or complied with in a merely tokenistic manner). Today, therefore, the question is not whether consultations and appeals to public participation are on the menu but rather whether the specifics of the process have a significantly democratic effect.

A 1969 text read by generations of urban planning students provides commonly used standards by which to measure not the presence but the quality of community consultations: Sherry Arnstein's *A Ladder of Citizen Participation*. Summarizing it will help guide this chapter. Arnstein studied various American consultation processes then in vogue, around such issues as urban renewal projects and national infrastructure plans. From a varied sample, she came up with eight categories, only three of which actually empower citizens. These are "citizen control" (a pipedream, except perhaps in tiny projects), "delegated power" (which one sees when a settler colonial state delegates power over a certain space or issue to Indigenous representatives), and what she calls "partnership", meaning joint administration. Again, the Indigenous politics context provides some good examples of co-management, in New Zealand and Canada in particular. While not the norm, in Canada some national parks have had their governance transformed by the adoption of co-management, joint administration structures.

Arnstein's next three categories are said to be versions of 'tokenism': 'placation', 'consultation', and 'informing'. Most infrastructure and urban planning consultations are indeed mere "consultations" in Arnstein's sense, meaning that the project has already been defined and the community is consulted only in respect to minor details (such as the shape of a new green space or the colour of a new building, to pick two examples from my own citizen experience). There is no sharp line dividing consultation from mere information, especially at virtual public meetings that are run as webinars and hence literally silence attendees – a format that was popularized during the pandemic but is unlikely to be completely abandoned in favour of more unpredictable in-person public consultations. The final two categories, labelled as 'non-participation', are 'therapy' (where officials or experts try to cure locals of their perceived backwardness) and 'manipulation'.

Besides Arnstein's ladder, which remains useful not only for infrastructure consultations but also in other areas (e.g. educational institutions consulting their students), I would suggest one additional tool for citizen groups trying to hold governments and private companies accountable.

Journalism students are taught to always begin by asking who, what, where, when, and why: these are also the questions that should be asked of every community consultation/citizen engagement process. **Who** is organizing the consultation? **What** is up for discussion, and what is left in the background, perhaps by being labelled a commercial secret[3]? **Where** are the consultations held, and how do the venues chosen skew participation? **When** are they held? Meaning not only weekdays vs. weekends but also, more importantly, whether they're held before the project takes shape (before a request for proposals is issued) or only after the main contractor has been identified. Finally, **why** is 'the community' being consulted? Only to comply with legal requirements? Or is there a genuine interest in learning how people see their community's present and future interests?

We will go over these five 'w' questions in turn.

Who?

From 2017 to 2020, I diligently read documents and attended public meetings concerning a 'smart city' project in Toronto proposed by the Google affiliate Sidewalk Labs.[4] The first few public meetings organized to inform the population and collect their views were organized by and run by Sidewalk Labs, the private-sector firm. As soon as I entered the large convention hall, I noted with surprise that neither the local city councillor nor the senior city staff I was used to seeing at public meetings was on the stage, as happens in the city's numerous development consultations. A key element concerning the 'who' of

---

3　There are categories of legal secrets beyond those covered by copyrights or patents; 'trade secrets' is one such category. Protecting trade secrets can mean that a corporation, such as a tech company with plenty of intellectual property in software, can legally make certain facts about the project invisible to the public.

4　For several analyses of the Sidewalk Labs project, see Mariana Valverde and Alexandra Flynn, eds., *Smart cities in Canada: digital dreams, corporate designs* (Toronto, ON, James Lorimer, 2020).

that consultation emerged only in retrospect for me. Only after I had become more informed about data mining and about Google in particular did I realize that the many hundreds of people who attended, including me, were actually unpaid rats in Google's labs. Having educated myself on data mining, I came to realize that every little yellow Post-it note on which we were asked to write a comment probably ended up as 'training data' feeding Google algorithms.

Google, of course, is a very special actor: but the larger lesson about data, including negative comments, being a key resource for firms' PR and marketing campaigns is applicable in other contexts. The project may not be modified to respond to criticism, but the communications professionals may well then produce and disseminate information that counters the concerns bubbling up from ordinary people.[5] That is only one of the many reasons why public entities are in most jurisdictions charged with the task of consulting citizens. The other, more principled reason is that it is only public entities that are accountable to that public. Corporations have no such duty and only respond to public pressures if their bottom line demands it. The fact that many public agencies carrying out infrastructure projects are run by managers who come from the private sector and are used to corporate methods including withholding as much information as possible from the public means that the public agencies often act as if they are private for-profit corporations in regard to consultations.

What

Another example from my citizen experience concerns the large public transit agency Metrolinx's plans for a whole new set of subway tracks and stations in my Toronto neighbourhood. Metrolinx has held some public meetings (limited to webinars with little time for public input) and has mailed flyers claiming to be open to comments. But it quickly became clear to my neighbours and me that the agency was not open to giving any consideration (even through the tokenistic

5 An example of this very tactic appeared in my mailbox as I was editing this chapter August 24, 2021: the powerful transit agency Metrolinx paid to produce and distribute a 12-page, full-colour flyer designed to calm the fears expressed by numerous citizens who had previously received a 'dear owner' letter imposing onerous conditions on properties in a very expansively demarcated 'transit expansion corridor', such as compulsory removal of porches, sheds, or hedges that in the opinion of Metrolinx impede transit works. See the community-based website www.savejimmiesimpson.ca for more on this story.

categories named by Arnstein) to the community's proposal to have most of the line buried (it is scheduled to be buried most of the way, but not in the 1.6 km that includes my house). Even when city council asked Metrolinx to release cost calculations for burying the line so one could compare costs and benefits, this did not happen. Metrolinx was not consulting on whether the line should be overground or underground, clearly. (In the summer of 2021, the agency reiterated it would not produce a cost estimate for an underground option).

Elsewhere in Toronto, Metrolinx is planning a subway train storage facility in the current site of one of the largest halal grocery stores in the country, one that they admit is a key community resource. There the agency is only interested in discussing the details of having the store move to another site but without consulting on the expropriation (compulsory purchase). So both the expropriation and the particular site for the facility are taken as set in stone, not open to any public debate. Unfortunately, citizens, at least in my many years of Toronto experience, tend to attend community consultations in good faith, responding to the requests for comments made by the proponents of the work without standing back to ask why only certain details are put forward for consultation and others are left out.

Another typical example of taking the 'what' of the consultation as wholly within the discretion of the infrastructure sponsor in question is visible in the secrecy that surrounds the financing of buildings. My university routinely shares drawings of imaginary new buildings within the university to get input on the design. Even on that limited scope of consultation, their responses fall squarely within Arnstein's "placation", in my extensive experience.[6] By blackboxing the 'what', as in 'which of the many pressing space needs will be met by the university?', the question of whether future student tuition fees have been promised to whoever is lending the money upfront is treated as off limits. But the fact is that in the extensive downtown campus of the University of Toronto, new top-of-the-line buildings have been almost without exception built by and for various professional faculties whose students pay far higher tuition than liberal arts students.

It is very difficult to challenge the 'what' is up for consultation given that infrastructure sponsors are everywhere used to presenting plans

6 Readers interested in my mini-research projects looking at the university as a developer can consult the website of the team project, "Discovering University Worlds", universityworlds@utoronto.ca.

and soliciting input only on certain highly delimited issues, just as focus groups run by marketing firms only solicit input on particular questions provided ahead of time by the corporation in question.

Where

Before COVID, public consultation and information meetings were usually held in places such as church basements and school gyms (or sometimes in hotel ballrooms, but those are rare occasions). Only certain people are familiar with and comfortable in these venues: the folks I call 'the retired schoolteacher demographic', basically. Young people, low-income tenants, recent immigrants, working mothers, people in precarious or shared housing – there are many groups that either for practical reasons or else due to cultural exclusions (e.g. a lack of interpreters even in communities with large numbers of newcomers) are highly unlikely to show up. Further, many planning laws give those who own or occupy properties very near the property being developed special credibility – whereas those who might benefit in the future but are not present nearby (such as currently homeless people or future immigrants) are excluded at all stages.

These exclusionary practices can be challenged. In the early 2000s, I was part of a community group concerned about local gentrification and its exclusions, called Planning South Riverdale. The city of Toronto was at the time conducting a planning study of the main commercial street in our area, Queen Street East. Having noticed how many high-end shops and restaurants had replaced more workaday outlets, we set up our own consultation, one that ran parallel to what the city was doing. We sent facilitators to venues such as a health centre programme for older Chinese Canadians, a women's shelter, and a halfway house for street-involved men. By going to the spaces where marginalized citizens feel and are at home, we made an effort to capture their experience of feeling driven out of the neighbourhood by the closing of shops and other venues catering to low-income people. Unfortunately (and predictably), we wrote a detailed report that included not only the consultations with people but also a careful mapping of businesses along the main commercial street, showing the very high degree of commercial gentrification that the city study did not capture. Local city planners claimed to read our report, but it did not end up in the official record.

Through the exercise, we found that the 'where' and the 'what' of consultations can merge: although city planners had used appropriate equity language when told about our parallel consultations, the scope of their study, which was the only official one, excluded socio-economic factors: it was purely architectural, it turned out. The hard data on commercial gentrification that had been gathered in person by volunteers was thus as irrelevant to the city's process as the focus-group findings. Planners, by law, only care about changes of legal land use, such as commercial to residential, and do not keep or use data on whether high-end shops and restaurants are replacing more affordable options.

When?

The temporality of consultations often goes unnoticed but has important effects. There are several dimensions of 'when'. One is the time of day/week for the consultations. Many working people do not have free evening time on weekdays but could make time on an occasional weekend afternoon – but the professionals who deliver the official information rarely make themselves available on weekends. One way of making consultations more democratic would be for organizers to poll the marginalized groups that are underrepresented in traditional consultations about when and where they would prefer to attend.

Further, there is the seldom addressed issue of whether citizens are included in infrastructure **planning** as opposed to being consulted only after the plan is drawn up. I do not know of any jurisdiction where citizens are included from the very start, with the notable exception of participatory budgeting processes – since by helping to draw up budgets citizens are indirectly making infrastructure decisions. However, in most cases, participatory budgeting exercises are limited to a small portion of the total budget, in such a way as to confirm that expenses that are arguably excessive – say on police – but are seen as fixed, in part due to collective agreements but also in large part due to political inertia, will continue to be approved.

Officials and contractors and certainly developers might say it is not possible or desirable to include citizens in the preliminary blue-sky discussions about infrastructure plans. However, there are two types of civil society actors that are very often represented, and often sought out, by those who plan how to spend public money on infrastructure. One such actor is finance capital, whether embodied in local banks or pension funds or in transnational infrastructure funds. If a project is unlikely to generate a good 'return on investment' (that is, profits), it is unlikely to see the light of day. The second type of civil society actor often consulted before the public consultations are developers.

An example from the many 'worst practices' regarding citizen engagement in infrastructure found in China is the building of a new ring road around Changsha, capital of Hunan province. There the state expropriated a large area covering 200 m on either side of the future road, paid the original owners a fraction of the market price, and then sold the land to developers at a higher price. This was meant to generate the very income that would finance the road itself. (In China, municipalities are not officially allowed to borrow money, a rule that generates creative workarounds and questionable PPPs.) Developers were most likely consulted beforehand (in the West that is known as 'market sounding') but citizens were not. Of course, China has fewer avenues for citizen engagement than many other jurisdictions, but in a modified form, similar processes of temporally uneven consultation exist and have existed for decades. It is common for governments to keep infrastructure plans secret until expropriation notices are sent out, for instance, so as to not have to pay the higher price to incumbent owners that the future plans would warrant. On their part, major lenders (such as pension funds) do not need to attend public meetings or write plaintive emails to have their voices heard.

Why

If it is possible to answer with some confidence the questions of 'who', 'what', 'where', and 'when' in a particular instance, one is likely to already have a pretty good answer to the question of **why** the consultation is being done – for real or for show. But citizens of countries that unlike China have legislated requirements for environmental assessments and community consultations may still be deceived about the 'why', especially if they are not familiar with local consultation practices. Authoritarian and arbitrary decisions are easy to spot and denounce. Less easy to spot are moves made by corporations and/or public-sector agencies to 'go through the motions' and 'check the boxes'.

Unfortunately, there is no hard and fast rule that differentiates a genuine interest in learning from the community about its needs and desires (which does happen on occasion, it must be said) from the process of checking off boxes so as to be able to say, "We did consult". Citizens have to gain experience, get involved in a variety of projects and citizen groups, and learn to compare and contrast different governments and agencies in the same jurisdiction and in theory subject to the same legal rules. It takes much energy and time to become an active citizen, and by and large, the entities that plan and deliver infrastructure do not make that easy. A key issue that is rarely addressed in official documents, but is also surprisingly absent from many urban planning scholarly studies, is the fact that officials and private firm representatives are all paid for their work for and their presence at meetings, whereas citizens, even when properly consulted, have to do it on their own time and rarely have the research capacity and the political contacts that the powerful private firms that do most of the infrastructure projects take for granted.

Conclusion

An issue not raised by Arnstein or most scholarship since is that it may not be possible for citizens to arrive at an informed verdict (democracy or pretense?) on the community engagement process until the project is well underway. It may take time to see whether the project reflects people's concerns since talk is cheap (as in the case of the Toronto city planners with progressive notions who were happy to agree that equity is important and avoided giving the Planning South Riverdale accurate information about the very limited scope of the official study). Further, since citizens are rarely all in accord, it takes time to see if the realities of the project reflect the views and interests of some local groups but excludes or disempowers others. It is easy for proponents of projects to trot out a group that is not opposed to a project that angers most citizens, especially if some inducement has been provided behind the scenes.

Citizen participation in consultation is tricky at the best of times because the social, economic, cultural, and environmental impacts of infrastructure projects can be predicted to some extent but never with complete certainty. That is why it is crucial for citizen activists to familiarize themselves with prior projects in their areas. If a government agency refuses to commission independent project evaluations (as many do), refuses to acknowledge any past mistakes, and/or refuses to make existing studies, say by academics or official evaluators, public, it is very likely that the organization suffers from the common condition of anti-democracy. As Arnstein warned long ago, this condition is not treated by showing pretty pictures of imagined futures and appearing to be open to comments.

Chapter 4

Credit ratings

Today, many people like to know their personal credit scores. To do so, we can download apps that reproduce in a more user-friendly format the ratings that have already been assigned to individuals by one of the major credit-check agencies. The much-advertised new apps market themselves not so much as information providers but as tools to help people along in the elusive quest for self-improvement: the apps give helpful hints on how to increase one's score and promise instant re-calculation as soon as we have followed their advice. In that regard, the credit score apps emulate the popular self-monitoring apps that subtly or not so subtly nudge you to keep track of how many steps you have taken in a day, how many kilometres you have cycled, how many calories you have consumed, and so on.

The credit apps marketed to individuals are often multi-purpose. In these, one's credit score appears as one of several numbers or qualitative categories that together create the 'truth' about a person as an individual financial actor (as opposed to a corporate or government actor, about which more later). The North American Credit Karma, which not coincidentally is only available to iPhone or Mac computer owners, has a number of functions besides informing you how your creditworthiness has already been quantified by the giants of personal credit ratings, Equifax and TransUnion. People can sign up directly with either or both of these companies, but that is quite costly. The apps that one can download without prior payment are not exactly free, but as is the case throughout the sector (apps marketed to individuals) customers are not told how the personal information they 'voluntarily' provide is monetized — even though many consumers by now know, rather vaguely, how 'free' programmes and apps make their money.

Individuals do not commission major works, however. For current purposes, the credit ratings that matter are governments' ratings since

DOI: 10.4324/9781003254973-5

even in the case of privatized projects whose business model depends on future user fees, local or national governments or other public entities such as transit agencies are generally 'behind' the project, implicitly if not explicitly. But the world of sovereign debt and government credit ratings described in this chapter is not wholly disconnected from the novel methods for informing individuals about their financial profile by means of full-colour digital visuals that are inevitably accompanied by 'helpful tips' on how to improve one's score. We shall see shortly that just as individuals are divided into 'good' creditworthy citizens on the one hand and bad risks (including those too young or economically marginal to have a credit rating at all) on the other, so too whole countries are sorted into good or bad risks by a few powerful rating agencies in New York City. But unfortunately for global South citizens, unlike individual credit ratings, national credit ratings can't be quickly improved by following a few tips. This is the crucial difference between individual credit scores and national credit ratings.

The transnational system of sovereign debt that underpins the vast international disparities in the quantity and quality of infrastructures such as paved roads and electricity grids has a dynamic that individual governments cannot easily manipulate. The ratings whereby Wall Street directly or indirectly shapes the fate of whole populations are not subject to the kind of game-the-system moves available to savvy individuals who learn just which relatively minor changes in financial behaviour will give quick results. In other words: it would be very difficult if not impossible to build an app for central bankers and finance ministers that would do for their countries what individual 'credit score' apps and their helpful hints can do for enterprising and Internet-connected individuals.

The reality is this: wealthy countries with strong currencies can and do get large amounts of money cheaply and without having to post collateral (see the previous chapter on 'bonds'). On their part, poor countries with weak currencies pay a lot more to borrow money; and on top of higher interest rates, the lenders (often, the IMF) can and do impose very strict conditions (such as cutting the size of the public service or raising the retirement age to minimize public pension spending) that hurt local majorities but help the lenders, located mostly abroad, to realize their projected profits.

Nevertheless, the story of government credit ratings, and of the very small number of shadowy US companies that generate ratings accepted as the ultimate truth about a country, is not a static picture of an unequal capitalist world. It is a dynamic situation that can be characterized as a vicious circle (if one takes the point of view of the perennial losers, who not coincidentally are by and large former colonies of European empires.) In this downward spiral, losers are more desperate for loans than richer countries because they have greater infrastructure and other needs, but they also have limited fiscal capacity. If they raise taxes on the rich, the local bourgeoisie will engage in 'capital flight', and other than taxing consumption, a choice that amplifies inequalities, it is very difficult to tax most economic activity if work is largely in the informal sector. Already disadvantaged countries therefore cannot easily fund infrastructure projects on a 'pay-as-you-go' basis – that is, out of yearly government revenues. But at the same time, it is the weaker countries that have to pay much more for loans, both in money terms and in terms of loss of sovereignty.

Deepening the vicious circle, for many poor countries, if a progressive nationalist government contemplates refusing to go into debt again or considers refusing to make scheduled payments on the very high-interest loans that were heavily marketed to them some years earlier by 'global' financiers, these are not viable solutions. Individuals can clear the decks by declaring personal bankruptcy, and corporations can choose to go into legal nonexistence (often a temporary state for corporations, unlike individuals) through what US law dubs 'Chapter 11 protection'. (Unlike individuals, corporations can usually claim creditor protection even when they are not actually broke.) The ease of the move depends on the particular legal regime, but seeking 'creditor protection' often has positive financial consequences for corporations because certain creditors (such as the company's pensioners) have to bear much of the cost of the 'failure', while managers and board directors, having escaped negative effects on their salaries and perks through limited liability law, live to form another corporation another day.

Governments are not afforded the same possibilities to clear the decks and start again as corporations. It is well-known that former US president Trump presided over several corporate bankruptcies on his way up to the White House, but the US government cannot renege so easily on the huge debt it owes to various Chinese state entities. Countries that choose to stay out of the world financial system become pariahs. They are not only 'bad credit risks'; they are seen as deviant, primitive, and irresponsible and have to pay a high price for exercising their sovereignty diplomatically as well as economically.

For these reasons, the countries that are the losers in the international system of differential credit terms, mainly in the global South but at times also including Eastern and Southern Europe (notably

Greece), are worse off than the hapless low-income American home-buyers who lost their life savings in the 2008–9 financial crisis. In the last resort, US home buyers (or more accurately, mortgage holders) could and sometimes did choose to abandon the partially paid-for house without trying to recoup any of the investment. But a government can't decamp and find another territory to start a new nation-state. It is stuck in place, unable to move or to emulate the Trump organization by restructuring itself as a new corporate entity. And further, its agency is very limited: unlike individuals, who are in most legal systems not forced to pay their parents' old debts, national governments are legally burdened with the debts that previous governments incurred – even if the happy-borrower politicians of the recent past have been discredited and thrown out of office.

Countries thus have the indefinite, potentially eternal lifespan of corporations (unlike individuals), but they lack the legal tools available to corporations to restructure, claim creditor protection, and start again from scratch. And if a brave government tries to walk away from the state equivalent of their mortgage (sovereign debt), the penalties can not only bring down governments but also create widespread misery among the hapless population, as we shall see next in the case of Argentina.

Who measures government creditworthiness?

It was mentioned previously that in North America there are effectively only two companies producing individual credit scores, TransUnion and Equifax. These are able to gather huge amounts of data because every time we open a retirement savings account, apply for a credit card, for a mortgage, or for a car loan, we have to check off a box hidden somewhere in the wordy official document (typically two or three pages of very small print offered for our signature, which few people have the capacity to truly understand even if they take the time to read it). Checking the credit-check box gives our legal consent to having not only our bank accounts but also all other debts, past and present, made transparent to the credit score producers. And if we contemplate pausing along the way to consider whether we should consent, the helpful financial advisor sitting across the table hurrying us along will glance through the document and say, "You forgot to check this one box".

I have not been able to see examples of the papers signed by government officials when borrowing money for public purposes, so I do not know if they contain the same checkboxes. Most likely such checkboxes are not necessary because unlike individuals, governments cannot claim any privacy for their financial doings. But whatever the actual form of the loan documents, the most important precondition of any government loan, especially in the case of a poorer country, is a forced one-way transparency, where the borrower has to 'open their books' to the lender/creditor. (The US might be an exception to this; what the Chinese government knows or can know about the inner workings of public finance in the US is not a subject that can be investigated through public records.)

But another similarity between personal and government credit ratings is that just as credit card companies or auto dealers arranging car loans don't actually do credit checks themselves but rather rely on the ready-made credit scores produced by the all-seeing individual credit-rating firms, so too the major transnational lenders (including international bodies such as the Asian Development Bank, but also big US, British and European private banks) may do some investigating themselves – but by and large, they rely on the government credit ratings already produced by one or more of three big American credit-ratings firms: Moody's, Standard and Poor's, and Fitch. These three companies rate not only national governments but also subnational governments and public-sector entities. For example, in 2020, these rating agencies warned that the credit scores of many universities in the English-speaking world might fall due to a sharp drop in international student enrolments due mainly to pandemic restrictions). Of course, they also rate corporations, but that is less important for present purposes.

A 2010 study in the *Journal of Economic Perspectives* persuasively argued, in the wake of the global financial crisis, that the disproportionate authority that was and still is accorded to the ratings generated by these three companies is rooted in the deregulation wave that began in the Reagan era. The New York–based Securities and Exchange Commission, notably, cut down on its own research and essentially outsourced investigations of corporate doings and misdoings to the rating agencies.

A second factor that both encouraged lenders to use the 'big-three' ratings without question but also made the ratings less reliable was a little-noticed reversal of the traditional credit-rating agency business model. Agencies used to be paid by potential investors to generate ratings for bond or share issues, but lately, the agencies have been paid by none other than the very entities they rate.[1] That this striking conflict-of-interest business model was a major factor behind not only

---

1 Lawrence White, "Markets: the credit ratings agencies" *Journal of Economic Perspectives*, vol. 24, no. 2, 2010.

the 2008–9 financial crisis but also somewhat earlier meltdowns is the view now held by most independent analysts. The fact that the three big agencies had given Enron good ratings until five days before its 2001 bankruptcy is regularly quoted as a warning of the consequences of the conflict created by having rating agencies paid by those needing to be rated – as is the fact that all three agencies rated Lehman Brothers as 'investment grade' on the very morning of the Lehman bankruptcy in September 2008, generally regarded as the first salvo in the global financial crisis.

One response to the obvious and disastrous failures of the rating agencies (among financial regulators and within the US Congress) has been to add a few more agencies to the list of approved firms to dilute the power of the big three. Thus, eight or ten firms, some specializing in a sector such as insurance and others based in countries outside the US, were added to the list. Nevertheless, by 2019, the three big New York firms still had 90% of the global market. Moody's, perhaps the most important one, rates 130 governments, 11,000 corporations, and 21,000 public-sector debt issuers (such as the special purpose agencies that play such a large role in current infrastructure projects).[2]

A further structural defect in the rating process is that the firms that generate the all-important ratings have added new functions that make them even more dependent on their income on the entities being rated. Moody's, for instance, has hived off a large new sub-company, Moody's Analytics, which provides consulting services and even marketing advice to the very entities that are supposed to be objectively graded by the other Moody's branch.

The final point to be made about the rating agencies is obvious but is seldom even mentioned, much less analyzed, in the literature – namely, US and specifically New York–based financial-sector bias of the rating game. All three agencies of course hire personnel all over the world, but the key decisions are made in New York, the centre

---

2 In privately financed infrastructure projects, bonds can be issued by the entity or consortium that governments have allowed to build, finance, and often maintain the infrastructure. These bonds are separately rated, which can make the public-private model more rather than less costly. For example, for the largest transit project currently (2021) underway in Canada, the Eglinton Crosstown light rail project (LRT) in Toronto, the initial set of project-specific bonds were rated quite a bit lower than the regular government bonds issued by the government that commissioned and will ultimately own the project. Projects in countries regarded as financially weak, however, could easily have credit ratings that are higher than the government's rating.

of US finance, and by individuals who have a particular career, training, social networks, and share certain values. On Wall Street, there are many high-level managers who were born outside the US, but by and large, they have degrees from American universities and have been socialized into 'Wall Street' as a social institution. And as Karen Ho's ethnography of Wall Street shows, future investment bankers are not those who excelled in economics or undergrad business degrees; the Wall Street firms mainly recruit at Harvard, Yale, and Princeton, and philosophy BAs are just fine as long as the student has been previously certified as "smart" in the Ivy League sense of the word – a sense that includes family background, personality, and hobbies.[3] Their prejudices and opinions are not a representative sample of the notions held by a demographically representative sample of the world's population or even the US population.

A warning example: the Argentinian debt crisis

In the late 1980s, as Argentina was emerging from a nightmare military dictatorship, there was a renaissance of the kind of people-oriented populism that Juan Peron and his wife Eva had pioneered in the post-World War II period (I say 'people-oriented' to distinguish Peronism from Berlusconi or Trump populisms, which were openly business-oriented not people-oriented). Noises made by a progressive president about the way in which global North financiers used loans to global South countries to further both their profits and the power of their countries made major banks leery of Argentinian government bonds. Once the vicious circle of bad credit ratings and conditional loans that are monetarily expensive and harmful to national sovereignty started, it continued in a downward spiral. The IMF emerged as the new colonial sovereign, supervising the details of governmental plans to make timely payments. The IMF demanded (as it did in many countries in Africa and elsewhere) that certain fiscal and economic policies be imposed by the government on the people, policies aimed at reassuring international holders of Argentinian bonds (bonds that had become popular precisely because they bore higher interest for the holders than the low-risk, low-interest bonds from 'good' countries).

3 Karen Ho, *Liquidated: an ethnography of Wall Street* (Durham, NC, Duke University Press, 2009), especially Chapter 1, "Biographies of hegemony".

Argentina now became the IMF poster child – all the while making the people suffer.[4]

This continued until one-third of total public expenditures were needed just to service the debt. In mid-2001, a consortium of banks, acting for the now rather diffuse multitude of investors (e.g. global North pension funds that held 'emerging market' bonds as part of a risk-diversified portfolio), came up with a solution to avoid or postpone a total default. The solution, known as 'the megaswap', had foreign bondholders accept new bonds maturing later than the ones they held. Needless to say, the new revised-date bonds bore higher interest for the holders – which helped the creditors to accept the deal but only made the downward sovereign debt spiral worse. Things got so bad that at one point the president had to flee the national palace in a helicopter; several presidents then quickly succeeded each other, none of them wanting to take responsibility for the dire credit situation.[5]

By the end of 2001, the country had plunged into misery. Devaluing the currency, a move that often helps boost exports, mainly produced hardships since industrial and agricultural equipment became unaffordable, and Argentina's exports were mainly agricultural products, not finished industrial goods. Inflation shot up, and phenomena associated with dire poverty such as homelessness sharply increased. Retail banking became essentially impossible.

In September 2002, I made a short trip to Buenos Aires. Given the currency devaluation, I thought I'd buy handmade leather goods to bring as presents back to Toronto, but found that even major stores would not take credit cards. It was also impossible for me to withdraw funds from ATMs. I also found out that books published abroad – another purchase I tried to make – were impossible to find because dollars were required, but nationally published books also became a rarity because paper too was imported, or it would have been if the country had the dollars to pay for it. In my childhood during the Franco dictatorship in Spain, Buenos Aires, a highly literate and

---

4 In the 1930s, the worldwide Great Depression led to several countries suspending payments on their debt, including Bolivia, Peru, Chile, and Brazil (as well as Germany, plagued by hyper-inflation). But at the time, Argentina was fairly wealthy and did not join the defaulters club.

5 The ongoing tragedy of Argentinian sovereign debt has often been told. One detailed account that helpfully puts Argentina in global context is found in Jerome Ross, *Why not default? The political economy of sovereign debt* (Princeton, NJ, Princeton University Press, 2019).

cultured city, had been a publishing mecca for Spanish intellectuals; the contrast with 2002 could not be starker.

Argentina's struggles not only with indebtedness but with associated phenomena such as the blocking of imports and sky-high inflation rates have continued into the 2020s, with greater or lesser severity – not surprisingly since international lenders, whether global North banks or individuals unknowingly holding Argentine bonds in a mutual fund portfolio are still benefiting from the misery of the Argentinian people. (In my latest financial statement, I see that "Latin American markets" have recently done well in the mutual fund I hold through my credit union, though, of course, I have no idea what that line item actually represents.)

Infrastructure projects are nowadays generally undertaken only if certain financial conditions obtain, especially a good rating for the creditworthiness of the project. Global North governments could easily raise some taxes to fund infrastructure (e.g. gasoline taxes can be used to finance public transit), but governments at all levels now usually prefer to rely on private financing, which makes projects more expensive but punts much of the public debt into an electorally irrelevant future (30 or 40 years). But how can countries in the global South undertake much-needed infrastructure projects? They cannot easily raise taxes even if they want to, given lower salaries, many informally employed workers, and the long-standing tendency of local bourgeoisies to decamp or at least send their money to Miami or New York if any redistribution threatens. And if governments choose to borrow rather than pay-as-you-go out of tax revenues, devalued currencies and a dearth of local wealthy investors makes them dependent on transnational credit giants, from the IMF to private entities like Goldman Sachs. The vicious circle thus continues, aided and abetted by American-based credit rating agencies designed to serve the interests of global North investors, not the world majorities.

Critical legal scholars often eschew any financial information. And yet credit ratings, especially the credit ratings of sovereign debt and debt issued by subnational entities involved in infrastructure, are a fundamental aspect of infrastructure.

Chapter 5

'The deal'

In the 1980s, the American finance world was caught up in a gold-rush-style fever. The spirit of the time was encapsulated in the 'Wall Street' film character Gordon Gekko's mellifluous baritone pronouncement: "Greed is good". The Wall Street film came out in 1987, the same year as Donald Trump's bestselling book *The Art of the Deal* (which apparently was wholly written by a ghostwriter, but that's another story, another 'deal').

The Trump pop-business book is organized, as the title implies, into chapters that each cover a 'deal'. Six of these were actually debacles – failed real estate deals in New York City and failed casinos in New Jersey. But although between 1985 and 1994 Trump showed huge losses in his income tax returns (which likely meant he paid no business income tax, another story of another 'deal'), he rose to the White House in 2016 using the notion that unlike public servants and ivory tower experts, he was a successful businessman. Having projects fail to the point of bankruptcy did not seem to tarnish this image. This amazing ability to turn failure into success is not just a personal trait: it is in keeping with the curious practice in the infrastructure world of awarding prizes not only for innovative or highly successful 'deals' but even for the best bankruptcies (renamed 'restructuring deals').

Successful businesspeople and successful corporations narrate their success in terms of 'deals'. The world of infrastructure projects follows this corporate logic: both politicians and the firms engaged to make and run infrastructure assume that infrastructure naturally divides itself into a series of deals. In other words, the industry as a whole is built on the assumption that infrastructure is nothing but a series of separate 'deals'. Politicians rise to power on the basis of promising not a long-range, evidence-based plan, but rather one or two shiny and fashionable 'deals'.

DOI: 10.4324/9781003254973-6

Deals are the unit of infrastructure at every level. In the US, the most important 'deals' are local (often involving a coalition of businessmen and politicians). In France, an unusually centralized country, each president for the past several decades has chosen a single showy project in the capital, Paris, as a presidential 'deal' – the Pompidou centre being perhaps the best known of these.[1] Similarly, construction and engineering firms bidding for a project will rely on their collective resumes, which are simply lists of previous deals, as their qualifications.

That the scale of the single 'deal' carries inherent problems is well understood by practitioners. A recent example is the spectacular collapse of an elevated subway track in Mexico City, in May 2021, which caused dozens of deaths and many disabling injuries. Line 12 (referred to as 'the gold line' since no deal is complete without an appealing name) was rushed to completion for political reasons. Soon after it opened, inspections revealed that the subway cars that had been bought from a Spanish firm because they could be delivered before a key politician went out of office did not match the tracks, which were built to US, not European, specifications. And the actual construction was clearly rushed too, as revealed in a *New York Times* detailed investigation (published June 15, 2021). One of the many clues that, if followed up, could have prevented the disaster was that the metal rods that welded the concrete platform above to the steel structure below had been welded in without the outside ceramic covers being removed. The rods were also scattered instead of being carefully lined up for maximum support. Since some of the flaws were known, after the 2017 earthquake in Mexico City, the whole line should have been closed for rebuilding. But that would have diminished the political fortunes of both national and local leaders – the mayor of Mexico at the time of the original deal being none other than Andres Manuel Lopez Obrador, more recently elected president of the country.

Stories such as the Mexico subway disaster can be found in virtually every country in the world. Often the blame is laid at the feet of the politicians who used the projects in question to gain electoral favours, as well as politicians and civil servants paid off by corrupt construction companies. The particulars differ from place to place and country to country, but failed infrastructures can be found everywhere, as the

---

1 For a detailed study of a more ambitious but still presidentially led plan, see Theresa Enright, *The making of grand Paris: grand urbanism in the twenty-first century* (Cambridge, MA, MIT Press, 2016).

fascinating collection *Disrupted Cities: When Infrastructure Fails* shows.[2] It is important, however, to go beyond the investigative reporting of scandals to appreciate why spectacular failures are common and see that, contrary to much news reporting, corruption and political ambitions do not suffice to explain them. More systemic, less site-specific, and less newsworthy factors are also to blame. One such factor is what geographers call 'scale'.

As already argued in the 'credit ratings' chapter, the way in which major infrastructures are now financed – as separate 'deals' – has become such an important factor as to override people-centred considerations and evidence-based priorities in infrastructure decision-making, in democratic as well as non-democratic countries. When electoral considerations are superimposed on the myopic scope[3] inherent in current globally popular financing methods, one gets a toxic mix in which both the public and the private sectors have a built-in tendency to ignore the larger context, including the subsequent socio-economic effects of the choices made by infrastructure bosses. The politicians focus on a single vanity project or perhaps two because they only see the next election; on their part, the firms only see the next deal because as corporations their work is simply a series of deals. Nobody who counts is obliged to take a longer-term perspective or think about the broader geographic, social, and economic context. Longer-term effects, unanticipated or anticipated environmental and economic ill effects – all of those are reduced to mere 'externalities', not only for the corporations but also for the politicians, who will no longer be in power when many of the consequences are felt and noticed.

It should be recognized that both public authorities and the private sector appreciate the shortcomings of the 'art of the deal' as a model for infrastructure. In recent years, the phrase favoured by large infrastructure funders is 'a pipeline of projects'. This phrase, found

2 Stephen Graham and Simon Marvin, eds., *Disrupted cities: when infrastructure fails* (London, Routledge, 2009).

3 By 'narrow scope' I do not mean only the physical limits of projects (e.g. high-speed toll highways, single subway lines rather than systems) but also the limits of the scope of the contract through which important considerations (e.g. damage to the environment or the carbon footprint of a project) are either ignored or passed on to often cash-strapped public authorities. My colleague Shoshanna Saxe, Canada Research Chair in Sustainable Infrastructure, is making an impact in Canada with her research on the carbon footprint of the construction process, which can be extremely high even when projects are labelled as 'green' because they involve public transit.

everywhere in infrastructure corporate documents, may have perhaps unintended fossil-fuel connotations but serves in industry discourse to indicate a desire for continuity – though only as a series of 'deals' that are more predictable than single ones, perhaps by being forced to follow templates.[4] A 'pipeline of projects' is a phrase that indicates a desire to go beyond the single deal, but in a limited way, since what flows through the imaginary pipeline is not a single fluid substance but rather a set of 'deals' that are bound to be different no matter how tightly the financial and governance procedures are standardized.

Standardizing deals, deals rendered commensurable and even fungible through the metaphor of the oil pipeline, is as far as the current masters of the infrastructure universe are willing to go in the direction of long-range planning. Standardizing 'deals' – by cutting and pasting contract clauses and/or continuing to award contracts to a very small group of firms, which my empirical research has found are routine practices – certainly promotes efficiency at the scale of the firm or the sector, but it is clearly not the same as evidence-based, jurisdiction-wide or sector-wide planning.

The demise of long-range, jurisdiction-wide planning

In the 1960s and 1970s, urban planning changed a great deal. Influenced by 'small is beautiful' ideas, and by Jane Jacobs' in-person and in-writing campaigns against the 1950s trend of bulldozing whole neighbourhoods to build new highways in the middle of cities, urban planners became wary of the architectural and urban-design ambitions that had long been associated with the 'great man' theory of urban development. James Scott's book *Seeing Like a State*[5] became influential precisely because it reflected and empowered the new 1960s scepticism about the type of megaprojects that had been favoured for several decades in the US by the New Deal and the Eisenhower-era

4 The relatively new Canada Infrastructure Bank, which is meant to promote public-private infrastructure partnerships, uses the phrase 'pipeline of projects' routinely, so do major financing actors and government agencies elsewhere – e.g. Australia.

5 James C. Scott, *Seeing like a state: how certain schemes to improve the human condition have failed* (New Haven, CT, Yale University Press, 1998). Like Jane Jacobs before him, Scott mainly criticizes political leaders; he does acknowledge that the private sector too can 'see like a state', but on the whole, he's more critical of public than of private actors, possibly because of the focus on colonial or neo-colonial projects in authoritarian states.

federal highway programme, and in Europe by car-centric approaches to post-war reconstruction (such as the rebuilding of bombed-out central Birmingham in the UK).

'Seeing like a state' was nevertheless never as dominant in practice as in theory. James Scott's examples are well chosen, for effect, but they are not representative of infrastructure trends. For example, while in the US 'urban renewal' (correctly dubbed 'Negro removal' by many) divided poor communities by running commuter-oriented highways through them and demolishing many mixed-race and mixed-income districts around the country,[6] in the UK and Canada, and in continental Europe, urban renewal was far more limited in scope. In the UK, new public housing, arguably the most important item on the infrastructure agenda between the wars and after World War II, was usually built on the outskirts of existing cities. That caused its own problems, such as isolation and bad transportation, but few existing English urban communities were levelled by the 'seeing like a state' gaze of the welfare state, compared to the US. And in Montreal, Toronto, and Vancouver, the suburbs exploded but without destroying old urban districts – which declined somewhat until around 1980 but which within a few decades of World War II became more desirable and expensive than the suburbs.

As well as being limited by economic and real estate factors, the 'seeing like a state' gaze was often also constrained by political and legal realities. In the US, ambitious urban regeneration projects flourished alongside suburban build-out during the post-war period, but the extreme political fragmentation of local government in the US meant many grandiose projects were highly localized. Waterfront complexes oriented to tourists and professional sports complexes designed to lure suburbanites to the city for a few hours at a time were both very popular and remain so today.[7]

---

6 There are numerous case studies of US urban renewal, but one book of special interest to lawyers, which puts urban renewal in the larger context of the deep anti-Black racism of US law tools from mortgage contracts to urban planning, is Richard Rothstein, *The color of law: a forgotten history of how our government segregated America* (New York, Liveright/W. W. Norton, 2017).

7 On the extreme political fragmentation of urban and suburban life in the US, see Gerald Frug, *City making: building communities without building walls* (Princeton, NJ, Princeton University Press, 1999). On urban development politics in the 1970s and beyond the literature is vast – one good source is John Logan and Harvey Molotch, *Urban fortunes: the political economy of place* (Berkeley, CA, University of California Press, 1987). A very useful study for the non-specialist is Susan Feinstein, *City builders: property development in New York and London, 1980–2000* (Lawrence, KS, Kansas University Press, 1994 and 2001).

The realities of infrastructure planning and urban development were thus often far more localized and uncoordinated even in the golden age of Robert Moses' top-down grand planning than the 'seeing like a state' critique implies, even in the richest country in the world. Nevertheless, it is not inaccurate for scholars working in postcolonial and other global South contexts to complain about the unrealistic as well as the undesirable features of what is dubbed 'the modern infrastructure ideal'. If during the post-World War II boom public funds had flowed to municipalities and non-profits at the local level instead of being used to build gigantic river dams and grand city centres in national capitals, it is quite possible (though one can never prove it) that infrastructure needs today would be far less acute and that communities would likely suffer fewer social inequities and environmental problems.

Beyond 'seeing like a state': seeing like a shantytown?

The modern infrastructure ideal has few real-life examples to illustrate it. Perhaps the German train system – seen from Berlin, where the vagaries of Cold War history mean that there are two overlapping transit systems – can serve as a real-life situation that resembles the ideal. In Germany, train service extends to most or even all sizeable towns, and trains are fast, reliable, and affordable. Inside Berlin, urban transit is nothing less than fantastic. It's no wonder that many Berliners do not own automobiles.

Whether in transportation, in electricity provision, or in arrangements for drinking water and sanitation, the 'modern infrastructure ideal' aims to create large, integrated networks that are well built and well maintained and suffer few interruptions. In this paradigm, citizens can trust that the systems will be there for them – water will flow when a tap is opened, the lights will go on when the switch is flipped, and so on – and that if it fails, the problem will be quickly solved. Citizens can go through their day smoothly, going to work or to school or to visit family and friends, with few physical or economic obstacles.

Many large cities fail to meet the standards of the 'modern infrastructure ideal', even in the global North. Britain, for example, has experienced major problems with transportation both inside cities and between them. Notably, the privatization and fragmentation of the formerly unified 'British Rail' system have led to notorious difficulties for customers, despite the high prices being charged by the competing for-profit companies. Currently, the British government is committed to a long-term very expensive high-speed rail project, HS2 – perhaps rooted in nothing more rational than the envy Britons experience when riding on the Eurostar or using French TGV's – but the project, discussed at more length in the chapter on 'high-speed rail – is proceeding fitfully and slowly, and there is no certainty that the reality will follow the ambitious plan. In any case, the HS2 was planned as a separate transportation system, one that will if built exist beside and not within the current system or non-system.

But scholars from the global South have questioned whether the modern, Western infrastructure model that even England cannot live up to is in any case the ideal to which all societies must aspire. Ananya Roy, a Berkeley geographer working mainly on India, is one of many postcolonial scholars promoting diversity in infrastructure thinking.[8] Some influential white male scholars living in the global North have in turn questioned the 'seeing like a state' ambitions underlying many infrastructure projects and much everyday infrastructure thinking.[9] Stephen Graham and Simon Marvin, as well as Colin McFarlane, whose research is primarily in Africa, have shown that in the global North even the 'best' infrastructures are not of equal benefit to all, especially in these neoliberal times when the trend is for both private and public actors to create small-scale 'premium spaces' instead of looking after the needs of the majority in a particular jurisdiction.

A further point that is taking many scholars towards exploring alternative approaches to infrastructure is one made by Idalina Baptista in a study of electricity delivery in Mozambique. She highlights an issue already raised by global North infrastructure scholars – namely, that most funding and financing flows to new projects (new buildings, new subway lines) to the neglect of maintaining and repairing existing infrastructures. She then goes on to show, empirically, that the national electricity company in Mozambique has been forced to include in its own description of its 'system' the numerous 'informal' and even illegal arrangements that actually maintain the network. It is well-known that throughout the global South (in South America, for example) many households, even whole districts, tap into electricity lines informally and illegally (as do households in some impoverished

8 Ananya Roy and N. AlSayyad, eds., *Urban infrastructure: transnational perspectives from the Middle East, Latin America and South Asia* (Langham, MD, Lexington Books, 2004). See also Roy's numerous articles in planning and geography journals.
9 Stephen Graham and Simon Marvin, *Splintering urbanism: networked infrastructures, technological mobilities and the urban condition* (London, Routledge, 2001).

parts of US cities, incidentally).[10] But Baptista's ethnographic research found that to map the location of electricity metres in order to charge appropriate fees, only the residents of 'informal' settlements could provide the company with up-to-date information. Official maps were insufficient and inaccurate, in part due to the self-built nature of some of the streets and houses but in part also because of the globally common habit of assuming that there is a sharp line dividing the legal from the illegal, the formal from the informal.

This type of empirical research on how infrastructure actually works, research that can help to upend the ubiquitous urban studies binary of formal vs. informal, shows two important points. First, infrastructure 'deals' today emphasize building new things, to the detriment of exploring ways to revitalize or repurpose existing material networks – the latter being possibly more environmentally friendly, as well as a cheaper way to meet needs. Second, maintaining networks, which is surely as important as building them (as the initial story about the Mexico City subway crash shows) is not a task that can always be monopolized by official personnel. In some cases, it is necessary to draw on the life experiences and local knowledge of people who both use and (usually invisibly) maintain infrastructures – and acknowledging and valuing this experience – and knowledge is always politically and ethically desirable, whether or not it helps in the provision and maintenance of infrastructures.

A point made in much of the global South literature on infrastructure and urban studies is, namely, that it is no longer useful to deploy a binary opposition between the official, legal, city on the one hand (the city of asphalt, as they say in Rio de Janeiro) and the informal, unmapped favelas or shantytowns inhabited by very large numbers of people, often the majority of a city's population. A special issue of the renowned journal *Urban Studies* is devoted precisely to challenging the formal vs. informal binary that has dominated much urban studies scholarship in the global South.[11] It is of course important to recover the experiences and voices of those who do not have access to modern, well-constructed infrastructures and are indeed living

10 Idalina Baptista, "Electricity services always in the making: informality and the work of infrastructure maintenance and repair in an African city" *Urban Studies*, vol. 56, no. 3, 2019.

11 See introduction to the special issue by Colin McFarlane, "Thinking with and beyond the informal-formal relation in urban thought" *Urban Studies*, vol. 56, no. 3, 2019, 620–3.

an extra-legal life, as urban anthropologists have long done. But the binary formal-informal ought not to be taken up in infrastructure studies, given that it has been shown to be problematic both empirically and theoretically within urban studies.

Conclusion

Recent critical scholarship, especially that focused on global South spaces, can help both practitioners and scholars get beyond the unhelpful binary oppositions that have dominated infrastructure plans – namely, formal city vs. informal settlements and the site-specific deal vs. the pursuit of a perfect network of integrated infrastructures fully occupying a whole jurisdictional space.

The fact that the lived reality of infrastructure often belies these binaries could also lead to challenging what one could call the fundamental binary of both urban studies and infrastructure studies, which is that of 'the North' vs. 'the South'. Even formal spaces in cities in the global North often show much decay, outside of the 'premium spaces' frequented by tourists and privileged consumers, and similarly, there are many privileged spaces in global South cities where residents can rely on taking a shower and turning on the lights every day. And if there is a North in the South and a South in the North, as is increasingly evident, perhaps doing without the North-South binary could be helpful in promoting careful research that begins with people's lives including their daily encounters with and needs for infrastructure.

How could citizens and policymakers begin to think about infrastructure needs differently? I would argue that instead of countering the site-specific and short-term logic of the 'art of the deal' by spreading the gospel of the 'modern infrastructure ideal', it may be better, and certainly more realistic, to undertake democratic infrastructure planning, including carrying out community needs assessments to guide infrastructure decisions. Democratic infrastructure planning would utilize the experiences and the knowledge of local conditions possessed by ordinary citizens, especially those in poorer areas, in order to plan for and build sustainable infrastructures that may look modest but that may improve people's lives more than showy new bridges or hydroelectric dams.

Chapter 6

High-speed rail

During the COVID-19 pandemic, air travel, within and between countries, declined precipitously. Forced to stay put, many people began to reconsider their travel habits, in part by considering their personal responsibility for the climate crisis. Airlines may build back their customer base post-pandemic, but flying, and the associated activities of mass tourism and frequent business trips, may never return to the levels they reached in the early twenty-first century.

High-speed rail has been the top iconic mode of travel for some decades. Its eco-friendliness is one of the reasons why it remains the paradigmatic emblem of modernity, efficiency, speed, comfort, and environmental awareness all in one. However, with a few exceptions, in most countries of the world, including the US and the UK, such travel has been more of a dream than a reality. Enter the slogan, popular on both sides of the Atlantic, of 'build back better'. In keeping with this spirit of the times, the key element in the UK government's ambitions for a quick social and economic recovery – post-Brexit as much as post-COVID-19 – is precisely an ambitious high-speed rail project: HS2. (The Channel Tunnel Eurostar trains to Brussels and Paris that have long drawn admiring glances from passengers dependent on regular British trains have been retrospectively dubbed HS1).

In this chapter, HS2 is used as the main example of both the promise and the perils of an important current infrastructure fad, high-speed rail, which in turn functions in this book as a case study in trends in transportation infrastructures. High-speed rail is an infrastructure whose projects require building expensive, all-new, dedicated tracks that are flatter and straighter than existing tracks, and hence require extensive new earthworks and land expropriations (compulsory purchases). The chapter's main aim is to question the 'myth' of high-speed

DOI: 10.4324/9781003254973-7

rail (myth not in the sense of a false notion but in Roland Barthes' sense of a real thing that has acquired a strong ideological weight[1]).

In more practical terms, the myth of high-speed rail can be critically examined by considering the 2020 minority/dissenting report on HS2 presented by Labour peer Tony Berkeley after he was cut out of the official Ministry of Transport HS2 report process. The short dissent, which sheds much light on infrastructure planning generally, raises the fundamental issue of whether it is worthwhile spending huge amounts of money and disrupting countless communities and habitats in order to provide brand-new 'premium' travel choices – instead of renovating and retrofitting existing rail networks, including not only engineering works but also financial and managerial reorganization. Lord Berkeley's brief report does not explicitly mention the possibility of reversing some of the privatization and fragmentation of former national networks that took place during the height of neoliberalism in Britain, and the great decline in quality and affordability of domestic rail travel that was the result, perhaps not of privatization as such but of how privatization was implemented. But Lord Berkeley's dissenting report is particularly useful for this book because it questions not so much the specific choices usually targeted by opposition politicians and auditors-general (contractors chosen, bridges built or not built, etc.) but rather the big picture: the initial choice to pursue an extremely expensive and extremely disruptive brand-new infrastructure instead of taking a close look at communities' infrastructure needs and at the state of the existing infrastructure.

In the previous chapter, on 'the deal', it was mentioned that many global South scholars are questioning the modernizing Eurocentric 'modern infrastructure ideal'. It seems that Lord Berkeley, and probably many ordinary Britons as well, would be willing to listen to their insights. Whether 'build back better' should mean putting vast public resources into just one or a few grand projects, as opposed to providing ongoing support for more modest improvement projects that are locally planned, is an important question.

The story of HS2 is relevant around the world. One reason is that Thatcher-era Britain witnessed the most radical assault on an adequate if workaday nationally owned rail network of any advanced capitalist economy (the US never had a real national rail network to dismantle, while countries such as Germany, France, and Spain only went partway

---

1 Roland Barthes, *Mythologies* (London, Jonathan Cape, 1972).

down the neoliberal road, in regard to rail travel). Hence, the current debate about whether the British government should put so much of its energy and money into the HS2 – a debate that in some ways covers or hides from view the long-running political argument about a potential renationalization of essential infrastructures – is informative for other countries that have also experienced a shrinking of state-owned enterprises and a decline in state-wide planning, and that are, to some extent as a consequence of the pandemic, wondering if the Thatcher-Reagan-neoliberal enthusiasm for privatization went too far.

Furthermore, this chapter will allow an exploration of something not covered elsewhere in the book: the symbolic power of infrastructure – that is, the symbolic power of both actual infrastructures and of the rosy representations produced by public infrastructure authorities and by the private firms that they hire, images routinely reproduced in the media without comment on the propagandistic aspects of the drawings and photos.

Previous chapters focused to a large extent on the political economy of infrastructure planning and delivery, which requires research and original analysis since political aims as well as financial details are generally hidden or disguised in official press releases and in politicians' speeches. The political economy of infrastructure planning and delivery, including the legal tools that structure and silently standardize 'deals', is obviously in need of independent explanation. That was the overall goal of the earlier chapters on audit, bonds, and credit ratings, where financial techniques that are intertwined with legal procedures in the making of infrastructure projects are discussed in such a way as to encourage citizens of theoretically democratic countries to use their agency in a reasonably informed fashion, in regard to projects in their localities. Large and expensive projects need more than bankers and corporate lawyers; they also require political and hence popular support. Such support, in countries whose governments are subject to electoral pressures, can only be secured if the projects are made to look literally appealing – in aesthetic and cultural terms, as well as in pragmatic terms, such as travel time and carbon emissions.[2]

2 Readers are invited to Google images of whichever major infrastructure project is being planned or built in their jurisdiction and consider the 'reality effect' (to use a term from film studies) of the appealing, noise-free and dust-free photos of future elegant spaces and structures. (For British readers, images are easily available online of the planned makeover of Birmingham's Curzon Street station, as well as the planned new HS2 station with the unlovely name of 'Interchange'.) Landscape architects play

Urban studies scholars have long studied the combination of features that made Baron Hausmann's nineteenth-century radical makeover of Paris streets and neighbourhoods succeed; they have also documented the shift, from the 1960s onward, to a 'small is beautiful', Jane Jacobs-inspired suspicion of very large projects, at the urban scale. But while infrastructure is a huge part of urban life, it is also a large part of the life of the nation – especially since the invention of railways, canals, and, later, airplanes, all of which cross many local spaces and change them irrevocably, including suburban and rural areas.

Scale matters, as legal geographers have long pointed out, and national projects require as much critical attention as the city-specific endeavours investigated by urban studies and planning scholars. In this respect, both the HS2 and, on the other side of the Atlantic, signs of a possible President Biden–led massive infrastructure plan, highlight the key role that infrastructure, especially transportation, has played in national life, however intermittently. Some projects meet local needs and are best planned locally, but small is not always beautiful: electricity grids and intercity trains, among other needs, require planning at a different scale than that of micro-neighbourhood improvements. And today, it is becoming increasingly clear that cities do not have the fiscal or the legal resources to truly halt climate change. Even local projects, such as flood protection measures to safeguard coastal cities, usually require national support and funding. We may perhaps be at the start of a new age of national planning.

When governments pursue ambitious New Deal–style national infrastructure plans, something that has rarely happened over the past 30 years in Europe or North America[3] but could in the post-pandemic

a rather small role in most infrastructure projects but are usually charged with producing the pictures of the imaginary future that arguably play a key role in soliciting public support. Cultural studies scholars routinely cite Walter Benjamin's famous writings on iron building structures, urban arcades, railway stations and so on, but there are not so many studies of the cultural and aesthetic dimensions of today's signifiers of progress and modernity. For one such study, see Shannon Mattern, *A city is not a computer: other urban intelligences* (Princeton, NJ, Princeton University Press, 2021).

3 In many Asian and African countries grand infrastructure projects are currently underway, often financed and delivered by Chinese companies with close links to the Chinese state. There is an incipient literature in English on the Chinese government's "Belt and Road" initiative, although politically independent case studies are scarce. The insights offered in this chapter likely do not apply to Chinese-backed large-scale infrastructure, but the arguments in the first three chapters likely do, insofar as lawyering and financing are not tremendously different in China than in the West.

era be turning into a trend, the drawings of pretty new parks and grandiose new structures that fill the pages of infrastructure reports are as important as the dollar figures – or perhaps more important – since meaningful financial figures are usually kept away from public eyes. The appealing images found in both private sector and government project announcements incite viewers, who are for the most part voters, to lend their support to plans whose details are rarely properly disclosed, even if the general public were in a position to appreciate and evaluate them. The private firms that dominate large-scale engineering, major infrastructure construction, financial services, and large-scale design/architecture work are, like any corporation, keen to sweep possible difficulties under the carpet. And distributing literally glowing images of a near future that can be brought about by decisive political action is likely to help bring the decision in question closer while conveniently drawing people's attention away from unintelligible contracts and hard-to-locate financial details. Cultural studies scholars interested in the ways in which Barthes-style myths function to elicit an emotional attachment to government infrastructure plans would do well to peruse the websites of both government infrastructure agencies and the handful of global firms that carry out such large-scale works as container ports, railways, and toll highways. Everything shown is shiny and new; always imperfect humans are either absent altogether or reduced to cartoon figures; no construction debris, dust, or noise is visible/audible. And so that the audience can feel they can have their infrastructure cake without destroying nature, a few highly domesticated green spaces usually break up the grey ultramodernity of the buildings or facilities being imagined. The HS2 documentation, for instance, contains idyllic images of creeks flowing, seemingly in their original natural course, under very new bridges that carry the ultramodern and ultrafast trains of the near future. How the brand-new bridges were built without disturbing or destroying the streams being shown is a question that only committed environmentalists or left-wing cynics would ask. For most viewers, seeing is believing, even if what is seen is an artist's drawing.

A curious feature of the vast image-reliant marketing component of the infrastructure-enabling field is that the government agencies and ministries that are supposed to be ultimately in charge, since they ultimately foot the vast majority of the bills, use the same representational practices as their contractors. The recent HS2 'Corporate Plan' for 2021–24 (issued in mid-2021), for example, is indistinguishable from what a for-profit private corporation generates, in form as well as in substance. A large high-resolution image of the HS2 train parked at an imaginary station and literally glowing is credited to none other than Alstom, the French corporation that specializes in light rail and high-end transit. That HS2 is a government entity charged with commissioning major public works is not at all apparent from its communications. And that forgetfulness of its public nature is not a specifically British or a Conservative characteristic. In Canada, Infrastructure Ontario (created by a long-running Liberal administration) and Partnerships BC (created under a conservative regime but continuing today under a left-of-centre government) use strikingly similar images and phrases.

Many national governments were already, before COVID, putting both financial and marketing resources behind high-speed rail. In the US, since President Bill Clinton's day in the early 1990s, Democrats have been attempting to foster high-speed rail at least between some cities. In July 2021, the Biden government announced that a large sum would be made available to build California's planned high-speed rail network, starting with a San Francisco to Los Angeles line. Washington's intermittent efforts on this file, however, have been hampered by the fact that the vast majority of transportation in the US is either in private hands or else controlled by municipal-, regional-, or state-level public agencies. There is a national line, Amtrak, but it does not serve most of the country.

Not coincidentally, the countries that have the best and largest high-speed rail networks have national passenger rail monopolies or quasi-monopolies. Germany has long had a serious, extensive, and unified national rail network; Spain went through a moderately neoliberal turn when in 2005 it divided the national passenger rail company, RENFE, into two, one owning and managing stations and services and another in charge of tracks and trains but eschewing outright privatization; on its part, France has long been running trains and services all over the country under the welfare state–style banner of SNCF, a national passenger rail system that is truly a system. In regard to China, which is heavily investing in all manner of infrastructure, including passenger rail, the line between the state and the for-profit sector is very blurred, but the central state has certainly been the prime mover of high-speed trains, as well as the novel 'maglev' (magnetic levitation) superfast trains. (Incidentally, the maglev trains may have been thought of as pilot projects but have turned out to be isolated examples of a futuristic but exceptional type of infrastructure, available to a very small fraction of the population.) Japan, in turn, has long taken pride in its state-supported 'bullet trains'. In turn, the passenger rail network in India that employs the largest single workforce in the world was designed and built from the top down by British colonial authorities;

its unified and statist origins made it quite compatible with India's post-independence socialist period.

All along, many poorer countries have never had a functional national passenger rail network. In general, passenger rail, like electricity service, is only truly functional when there is an extensive network; passenger rail does not suit what Chapter 5 called 'the art of the deal'. In some cases, isolated examples of good public train service that could have been the beginning of a nationwide system were abolished at the height of neoliberalism for ideological reasons.[4] The current stirrings in parts of the global North of a desire to 'build back better' by investing heavily in national passenger travel may thus find echoes in global South economies – though perhaps only insofar as the economic devastation of both COVID-19 itself and its restrictions, mitigated in the global North by plentiful vaccines, may allow any major public investments.

As already intimated in the chapter on credit ratings, even if infrastructure construction is a worldwide trend, how infrastructure will be planned and financed, and who the infrastructure will mainly serve, will certainly be very different in countries with large tax bases and good credit ratings vs. poor countries.[5]

When travel is more than movement: shifting symbols of modernity

In every period of modern economic development, a particular mode of travel has been favoured culturally: an emotionally imbued mode of travel seen as representing the era or, better yet, the near future. The 1830s and 1840s saw the rise of railways. Though for freight purposes, these were not always competitive with canals (some of which were nationally planned and financed, others not), for passenger purposes, the new railroads were not only a symbol but also a very material harbinger of the physicality of modernity.

---

4 Chile's extremely mountainous terrain and linear geography are unsuited to national train networks along European lines, but there was a good public train service between Santiago and the nearby town of Valparaiso that was abolished by the Pinochet regime and has yet to be revived, although the tracks were never removed, and in Valparaiso itself are used by a small-scale local subway-style train.

5 The huge amounts of money in global infrastructure funds and pension funds that like to 'invest' in infrastructure may, however, promote unsustainable indebtedness among some global South countries lured by the siren song of modern efficient infrastructure, especially if the World Bank and the IMF promote this type of expenditure.

George Eliot's most famous novel, *Middlemarch*, centrally features not so much actual trains (the novel is set in the early 1830s when railways were still in the planning stage) but rather the anxieties of English provincial folks about the new travel method. In Book 6, Chapter 56, we read that in the fictional town of Middlemarch, "railways were as exciting a topic as the Reform Bill [of 1832] or the imminent horrors of cholera. . . . Women both old and young regarded travelling by steam [trains powered by steam engines] as presumptuous and dangerous, and argued against it saying nothing should induce them to get into a railway carriage". The novel features lengthy debates amongst rural landowners about whether getting a good price for expropriated land would compensate for the horrors of the new invention – with rural characters debating whether the trains might make cows stop giving milk or birthing calves. On their part, medical doctors in the continent, as well as in Britain, hypothesized that the inordinate speed of the steam-powered passenger trains (the trains were certainly much faster than horse-drawn carriages) might induce, in humans, 'neurasthenia' and other nervous diseases of the Victorian bourgeoisie. Victorian anxieties associated with clunky steam trains may be coming back in a new guise, incidentally – the queen is said to have expressed concern that the racehorses of the British elite might be spooked by the proposed HS2 trains, which can go as fast as 250 miles per hour. The story may be apocryphal, but like many such attributions, it is revealing.[6]

Once railway travel had become normalized and rendered fairly punctual[7] (with Agatha Christie's detectives, for instance, treating the schedules of intercity trains as absolute forensic truth), rail travel lost its air of danger and became 'blackboxed', as actor–network theorists say. By the late nineteenth century, the hopes, as well as the anxieties, of modernity became fixed on another mode of passenger travel: the transatlantic liner.

As a matter of fact, the vast majority of transatlantic steamship passengers were low-income Europeans emigrating to the US or to ports such as Montreal and Buenos Aires, but steamship company marketing emphasized the luxuries available to first-class passengers in the hopes of

---

6 Mark Lawrence Wild, "All the queen's horses: statutory authority and HS2" *Legal Studies*, vol. 37, 2017, 765–85.

7 The rise of intercity train travel is often said to have been the impetus for standardizing times and synchronizing clocks across whole European countries. Prior to train travel, it rarely mattered whether a village town clock was five minutes faster than the next village's church clock.

increasing the number of tickets in all three classes. The sinking of the Titanic was thus a major event in the cultural history of modernity. But the famous sinking is also a key moment in the cultural history of transportation infrastructure, one that remains emblematic of the carefree lives of the European and American rich just before World War I. The way in which the ballrooms of the first-class passengers hide from view the miseries of the steerage immigrants continues to live on in contemporary stories, films, popular songs, and what we now call 'memes' (such as the phrase 'rearranging the deck chairs on the Titanic').

In the period after World War II, airline travel became infused with a similar mystique of speed combined with elegance. At that time, air travel was a rare occurrence, something exciting. I'm sure my family was not the only one to insist that we children dress up for the flight we took to emigrate to the US from Spain in August of 1967. I still remember the new green and yellow skirt I was wearing all through the very long trip, an unusual item in my tomboyish wardrobe.

In the golden period of airline travel, flights were expensive and hence unusual. But there was such glamour attached to the mode of transportation![8] There were no draconian airport security procedures; the food served by the solicitous and well-dressed cabin crew was good and served with proper dishes and cutlery; children were sometimes allowed to go into the pilots' cabin mid-flight; passengers were provided with free drinks, blankets, and other items they could keep. No wonder that the emblematic imaginary plane passenger was an elegant white woman resembling Jacqueline Kennedy.

Airlines began to expand their market well beyond the Kennedy set, however, in order to boost their annual revenues. By the 1990s, the majority of flights were cheap tourist flights in which people dressed down, not up, to travel, and drinks and even food had become either scarce or expensive or both. The air of elegance had vanished completely from the vast majority of flights by the early 2000s. A planeload of working-class English tourists on their way to an all-inclusive resort in Mallorca became the norm. On their part, airports became increasingly uncomfortable, especially when security measures and identity

---

8 While here I emphasize the cultural and symbolic power of specific modes of travel, bracketing their legal qualities, William Walters' work on 'viapolitics' shows that the mode of travel can have specific legal effects, as when countries ban arrivals by boat or treat them differently than arrivals by passenger plane. William Walters and Johann Arnason, "Migration, vehicles, and viapolitics: three theses on viapolitics" *European Journal of Social Theory*, vol. 18, no. 4, 2015, 469–88.

checks were severely ramped up in the wake of terrorist attacks. And the flight itself became uncomfortable unless one could afford to pay for business class or, on long-haul flights, first-class mini-lounges – through which the hoi polloi had to walk on their way out of the plane, getting the clear message that only the rich get to travel comfortably.

As of this writing, the airline industry is only starting to recover from the pandemic crisis, and there is great uncertainty about whether cheap crowded flights and the middle-class global North habit of taking frequent plane trips for both pleasure and business will return. But as mentioned at the beginning of the chapter, citizens in every part of the world are increasingly aware of climate change issues; further, many businesses found during the pandemic that they need not pay for staff travel because videoconferencing is more or less free. It is thus unlikely that passenger air travel will ever return either to its post-war golden age or to the later period of mass-tourism, steerage-style flying. Enter the high-speed train.

The lure of the fast, luxurious, and new

The first European high-speed train on dedicated tracks opened in 1992 in Spain in time for the Sevilla World Fair and the Barcelona Olympics. The new type of train was baptized AVE (a rough approximation of the initials of 'high-speed train' in Spanish), and it was marketed heavily in television commercials featuring, predictably, the soaring music of "Ave Maria". Currently, Spain has 900 miles of high-speed train (including routes under construction), very high by anyone's standards.

In earlier times, European premium trains, such as the famous Oriental Express, combined the glamour of international travel with the alluring air of luxurious cosmopolitanism. Such a train was a Grand Hotel on wheels, and the train wheels were in fact able to smoothly cross international borders. Premium train travel in Spain had been held back historically by the fact that the Spanish rail system had since the beginning used a different gauge than the rest of Europe: it would have been impossible for the Oriental Express to include Spanish cities on its route.[9] But engineers working for the Spanish state rail system

9   When I was a child in Barcelona, I was told by a teacher that the reason why Spain chose a different gauge than Europe for its train network was to prevent a neo-Napoleonic invasion of the country by means of troops on trains. This nationalistic myth was likely disseminated in order to hide questionable procurement and finance decisions, but for current purposes, the actual reasons for the gauge difference are not relevant.

developed an innovation whereby passengers could stay in their seats while trains at the French border, in both directions, had their under-carriages and axles manipulated to fit the 'foreign' gauge. Spanish trains could now go directly to Paris or Geneva, and, just as important, Spanish people could buy tickets for those trips from their national rail system. For a country slowly emerging from decades of dictatorship and of cultural as well as political isolation, the appeal was irresistible, even to those who could not afford a trip to Paris.

But the first Spanish flexible-gauge train was not the high-speed AVE. It was a train that used traditional tracks but significantly increased both speed and comfort, in part through airplane-like interior design and in part by mechanisms that greatly diminished vibration for pas-sengers. That rather unheralded innovation was named the TALGO. In the 1980s, it was widely used in high-traffic routes in Spain but lost its lustre when the AVE was implemented. Nevertheless, in recent years, many international customers (in Germany, Denmark, Kazakh-stan, Uzbekistan, Scotland, and Saudi Arabia[10]) have bought the newer versions of TALGO – perhaps because they unwittingly anticipated Lord Berkeley's critique of the previously cited HS2 project.

The TALGO represented a major improvement. It could go much faster and smoother than the old clunky trains, and the interior was air-conditioned and comfortable, and unlike the AVE or the HS2, TALGO trains did not need new infrastructures or specially built sta-tions. That has made the TALGO appealing to the operator of the regional train in the Pacific northwest that links Eugene, Oregon to Vancouver via Seattle. In Spain itself, the TALGO's allure faded con-siderably after the AVE was introduced and heavily marketed. But it may well experience a renaissance in the post-COVID era, perhaps especially in countries that never undertook the massive works (new tracks, much flatter terrain, new stations) required for high-speed trains such as the AVE.

A clue that suggests some fear and trembling among operators of the superfast trains that run on dedicated tracks is that in order to lure passengers back in the COVID-19 vaccine era, both the Spanish AVE system and the French TGV's operated by the SNCF invented something that does not require massive earthworks or expropriations: a "low cost" high-speed train. This turns out to be the same as the

10 The Spanish-built, high-speed trains designed to efficiently bring pilgrims to Mecca from other Saudi cities were the occasion for a major bribery scandal that resulted in the former king of Spain, Juan Carlos I, exiling himself to the Emirates in 2020.

existing high-speed trains but with a lot more seats and fewer amenities (e.g. no restaurant car, strict baggage limits). The French version is called "Ouigo" (perhaps meant to sound to Anglophone ears as 'we go'), while the Spanish version is called "AVLO", for 'AVE low cost'.

Central governments in France and Spain decided decades ago to create a new system of rail tracks dedicated to high-speed trains, so it makes sense that the managers in charge are now trying to keep those specialized assets going, even if that means turning the formerly luxurious high-speed trains into the equivalent of cheap-airline tourist class and risking losing the cultural prestige of the TGVs and the AVEs. For jurisdictions that never built the dedicated super-flat tracks and the extremely expensive tunnels and starchitect-designed stations that are de rigueur in the high-speed train business, however, it could be wiser to emulate the states of Washington and Oregon (or the train operators in Denmark) and look for suppliers that can offer comfortable and reasonably fast travel that can use existing stations and tracks.[11] This approach appears to be what the Canadian government has chosen, as seen in a summer of 2021 announcement about a projected 'high-frequency' (not high-speed) service linking the major cities in Ontario and Quebec, a service that unlike today's 'VIA' would not force passenger trains to wait on sidings for freight trains to pass.

The dissenting report on HS2 issued in January 2020 by the Labour peer Tony Berkeley (mentioned earlier) suggests that due to COVID-19 and other reasons (especially, I would say, though Berkeley doesn't, the government's perceived need to cater to Not In My Backyard (NIMBY) Conservatives through expensive changes, most notably burying the HS2 line for 64 miles through the Chilterns), the cost has greatly ballooned, perhaps up to 100 billion pounds sterling. As a result, the whole HS2 project is in question. Berkeley's dissent concludes that the project is "poor value for money". But more importantly for present purposes, he suggests that it might be far wiser to improve train service on regular tracks – which abound in Britain,

---

11 The perils of trying to build special stations or parts of stations for high-speed trains, together with the necessary tunnelling, are currently on display at London's Euston station. Suggestions are being made that the HS2 from Birmingham (and Crewe) will terminate at Old Oak Common station and not go into central London, despite the fact that rivers of money have been spent to (a) evict protesters from the tunnels at Euston and (b) expropriate and demolish several commercial properties immediately to the west of the current Euston station in preparation for a dedicated station next door to the current Euston.

including Wales and Scotland[12] – rather than follow the international fad and continue to sign multi-billion-pound contracts for new tracks and special stations with the multinational firms, most of them in continental Europe, that dominate that particular industry.

The myth of 'supply-chain' benefits

HS2's Corporate Plan for 2021–24, issued weeks before the government (in July 2021) stopped the process by which Parliament was to approve funding for the second phase (to Manchester along one branch and to York, Leeds, and Newcastle along another), declares that the HS2 project is a major brick in the wall of post-COVID-19 economic recovery. The spectre of Brexit is clearly haunting the corporate plan writers, even though the word is not mentioned. In fact, HS2 has signed some contracts with local suppliers and has furthermore given away a few thousand pounds to community-based environmental and/or social-benefit groups in an effort to blunt some of the extensive criticism. But the vast majority of large-scale contracts are not with small or even large domestic firms but rather with the kind of consortia that regularly earn the right to design and build and sometimes maintain the largest of infrastructures. The various consortia do include some British firms but also, usually in leading roles, specialized global firms mostly headquartered in continental Europe.[13] The Austrian firm Strabag (known among infrastructure geeks for its origins in building concentration camps for the Nazi regime), the Swedish giant Skanska, the French giant of "contracts and concessions" Vinci, and the French engineering firm Systra are set to reap profits from British public expenditures. (The geographic location of these firms' headquarters is rigorously unmentioned in HS2 communications, likely to support the Johnson government's stance on Brexit.)

12 Scotland was supposed to benefit from HS2 in the future, with lines to both Glasgow and Edinburgh planned at the outset, but currently, anything beyond the Midlands is in question. And Wales was never included in any plans, which has prompted the Welsh assembly to demand compensation payments.

13 The HS2 started to be planned well before the Brexit referendum, mainly during the Cameron government but to a small extent also earlier, under New Labour. One result of this is that a very detailed environmental assessment under EU rules had to be carried out prior to project approval (50,000 pages' worth). There has been important recent litigation to determine whether EU law still applies to various aspects of the HS2, as explained in the article cited in footnote 1.

The HS2 communications machine repeats that 95% of the firms that are getting contracts are based in Britain, but that is highly deceptive: any truly global firm will set up branches in countries where they have or they expect to bid for large government contracts.

Official HS2 statements repeatedly highlight the number of jobs created, which is in the thousands – but without mentioning how many of those are short-term construction jobs that will disappear once the work is either finished or abandoned. Other infrastructure agencies, by contrast, are forced by their political masters to separately count the number of construction jobs versus the much smaller number of permanent jobs created. Overall, contrary to the Brexit ideology of the Johnson government, what the HS2 managers call 'supply-chain benefits' are likely to be of much more financial benefit to large European firms than to British businesses.

One could go over more details while avoiding English-centrism. Most elements of the HS2 story, from the curious personification of the tunnel-boring machines (always described as "giant", even in *The Guardian*, and always named as if they were people, mostly with female names) to the mystery surrounding concessions and contracts at stations are exact replicas of elements visible in large infrastructure projects around the world. Instead of accumulating more damning details, however, we draw this chapter to a close with a few concluding reflections.

Conclusion: dilemmas of large-scale resource-intensive infrastructures

In every era, a particular mode of passenger travel has acquired a privileged mystique, from the original steam-powered trains through transatlantic liners to today's high-speed trains. As with every successfully marketed product, high-speed trains have a great deal of symbolic power and what auto salesmen call 'curb appeal', but they may not always be the best transportation solution.

Costs always increase along the way, whether in domestic house renovations or a new train line, but grandiose projects often lack an exit strategy or a hard limit to expense. In the case of HS2, heavy additional costs seem to have arisen from the decision taken to build 64 miles of tunnels under the Chilterns – an area that nevertheless voted Liberal Democratic in the early summer of 2021 after decades of solid Toryism: but financial details are very scarce.

If a project's costs rise steeply, politicians may try to limit overruns by lowering standards in places that have yet to be built and/or have less political leverage – perhaps cutting out whole proposed lines. However, if a planned rail network is no longer a network but only one or two isolated, stand-alone lines, its functionality declines precipitously. The HS2 was planned as an ambitious and geographically expansive new network – only occasionally connected to existing train services – but the usefulness of the London-Birmingham-Crewe line will be greatly diminished if it is built to the highest standards but in isolation.

A final point concerns the masculinist and neo-imperialist gaze that favours very large expensive projects built by large global firms supported by legions of top-drawer consultants and corporate lawyers over more modest projects that address the pressing needs of those currently underserved by infrastructures. This is not a phenomenon of the global North only: many governments in the global South have tried to be or appear 'modern' and advanced by spending large sums of public money on gigantic projects that may be useful but that wreak damage on the environment and on communities, and that have rarely if ever been democratically chosen by the population in question. That British prime minister Boris Johnson has chosen the HS2 as his own 'signature' project is in keeping with this way of politicizing infrastructure. Infrastructure planning that is democratic in substance, as well as process, is incompatible with the notion of 'signature' projects.

Chapter 7

Public-private partnerships

.

"Partnership" is one of the most overused words of our time. NGOs are often said to be 'partners' of governments, for example, but they themselves also claim to have 'partners', some of whom are major donors, while others are community-based agencies in the global South that 'partner' with larger more professionalized NGOs to carry out specific projects.

In the university world too, much is obscured by the knee-jerk deployment of the word 'partner'. Faculty members are rewarded, with status and prestige, as well as research funds, if they can demonstrate a large number of 'partners' – in increasingly unlikely locations. Once upon a time, researchers partnered with researchers at other universities or countries, but now granting agencies often expect academics to develop links to non-academic groups. In my own context, the Canadian national granting agency for the humanities and social sciences (and law), Social Sciences and Humanities Research Council (SSHRC), now routinely runs competitions for "community partnership grants". I naively assumed that this granting programme could be used by progressive academics who work closely with community groups, including those engaging in 'participatory research' by group members who are not academics (such as the work of my local group Planning South Riverdale, mentioned in Chapter 3). But I came across a successful grant application in which the 'community' partner was none other than a large and well-funded police department. Fuming at the prospect of seeing top police managers jetting off to conferences on crime and safety on Canadian taxpayers' dime, while critics of police violence working in actual community groups were largely ignored, I realized that if the word 'community' has had

DOI: 10.4324/9781003254973-8

its meaning expand to the breaking point, as many scholars have noted, so has the accompanying word 'partnership'.[1]

In the realm of infrastructure, as mentioned in the introductory chapter, the term 'public-private partnership' (shortened to either PPP or P3) has become a central 'keyword' of infrastructure planning. Indeed, it is difficult to find a project that, even if fully funded and ultimately owned and operated by the state, could not be made to fit into the fashionable term. So let us begin by trying to clarify some of the multiple meanings of the term.

It is possible to stick the label of 'PPP' on an old-fashioned contract for a particular good or service. Chapter 8, on 'smart cities', has a brief description of the way in which Big Tech vendors, such as IBM, sell software and hardware packages to municipal administrations under the purposively vague term 'urban operating system'. Insofar as those contracts involve continuing relationships such as maintenance and repair, one could call them 'partnerships' rather than just contracts. But there is no hard line between a traditional contract for a service or good (say, a government purchasing weapons or vehicles) and a 'partnership'. Importantly, the law does not help in this matter. The various arrangements that need to be assembled in order to build and run infrastructure are rarely if ever legal partnerships (such as what one finds in a law firm where the partners share income and share risks). Further, in business law, the term 'limited partnership' has a specific meaning, but none of the infrastructure projects I have either studied or heard about seem to be legally structured as legal business partnerships, limited or otherwise.

When researching a kind of public-private project proposed by a Google affiliate, Sidewalk Labs, for Toronto's waterfront, I saw that both sides of the 'deal' – the public agency Waterfront Toronto and the New York for-profit firm Sidewalk Labs – routinely used the term 'public-private partnership.' And yet, when my colleague Alexandra Flynn used her considerable legal skills to search corporation databases, the only actual legal partnerships she was able to find appeared to be mere subsidiaries of Google.[2] The mystery deepened as she and I attended several public

---

1 An insightful analysis of myriad local 'community partnerships' in the realm of crime prevention but relevant for other realms is Adam Crawford, *The local governance of crime: appeals to community and partnerships* (Oxford, Clarendon, 1997).

2 See Alexandra Flynn and Mariana Valverde, "Where the sidewalk ends: the governance of Waterfront Toronto's Sidewalk Labs deal" *Windsor Yearbook of Access to Justice*, vol. 36, 2019, 263–83.

consultation meetings organized by 'Sidewalk Toronto', a name, with a professionally designed logo, that seemed to refer to the 'partnership' between the tech company from the US and the local waterfront development agency. However, after much searching, we found that 'Sidewalk Toronto' had no legal existence whatsoever. It was a logo in search of a legal identity – or in search of nothing beyond a logo.[3]

Researching the legal underpinnings of a project involving the rebuilding of public housing on a large downtown site meant to become a 'mixed' community of both private condos and rebuilt public housing (Regent Park), my colleague Aaron Moore found that despite the constant reiteration of the word 'partnership' to describe the overall 'deal' linking the Toronto Community Housing Company and the private developer Daniels, in fact, there was no such thing, legally. In that case, the P3 that was much trumpeted by local actors turned out to be as nonexistent, legally, as Sidewalk Toronto. Instead, there were about a dozen incorporated mini-partnerships, each for a small section of the ambitious project. The first mini-corporation's by-laws were available on the housing authority's website. We wanted to see if any changes had been made in the later phases of the project – that is, whether the housing authority had made changes to the later phases given that early sales of condos had been very good. Since corporation by-laws are supposed to be public, we asked for them (agreeing beforehand that the financials could be redacted). The access to information quest ran for almost a year and ended with a successful appeal to the Ontario Privacy Commissioner, but for present purposes, what matters is that at the end of the chase, the by-laws of the dozen or so mini-corporations turned out to be virtually identical. Admittedly, many local observers thought that building private condos in the middle of a notorious public housing neighbourhood, and in the wake of the 2008–9 financial and real estate crisis, was very risky; hence it is possible that the city council would not have allowed a real partnership at the outset even if the housing authority had suggested it.[4] But the key point here is that as in the case of 'Sidewalk Toronto', both the public agency and the private

3   I asked one of the many young people wearing blue 'Sidewalk Toronto' T-shirts who was his employer, thinking he was likely one of the many master's students in local planning programs who are routinely hired to help with community consultations, but he turned out to be a New York–based computer engineer employed by Google.
4   Aaron Moore and Jordana Wright, "Toronto's market-oriented subsidised housing PPPs: a risk worth the reward?" *Cities*, vol. 69, 2017, 64–72. I was the principal investigator on the overall research project, but the case study in question was done by Moore and Wright.

developer constantly talked about 'the partnership' as if it was a single legal entity.[5] 'The partnership' did not exist, in either case.

Elsewhere, at my own university, a senior staff member told me that the university had never functioned, in its real estate ventures, by way of P3s but explained that a planned new student residence on the edge of campus, built from scratch on the site of an existing old building, would be the first venture to be such a partnership. Six years later, there is no new student residence – while the second-hand bookshop that had long rented the ground floor of the university-owned building remains shuttered.

The University of Toronto's lack of entrepreneurial zeal is admittedly unusual. PPPs of different kinds, in the sense of different legal and resourcing tools and normative ambitions of varying political hues, are now routine in campus planning. This seems to be especially true in the US, which due to the large number and the high prestige of numerous privately owned and operated universities, has been a more fertile ground for such 'partnerships'.[6]

But let us leave the rather unusual world of university real estate[7] and return to the more politically visible world of public utilities, public transit, and transportation.

Modes of public-private infrastructure deals

Among practitioners, P3s are divided into groups or rather placed under different acronyms. 'DB' refers to a relatively simple contract whereby a public entity (a government or a transit agency, say) decides to outsource not only the building of a new harbour or highway or train line, as public authorities have traditionally done (the B, also known as 'traditional public procurement') but also to outsource the design (D). Since DB and DB+ arrangements are common, one often finds architecture firms (large

---

5 The legal story became even more complex years after our study was complete. In 2018, the housing authority proposed that phases 4 and 5 of the overall Regent Park redevelopment be subject to a new tender; the competing developer, Tridel, was awarded the 'deal' in 2020.

6 A series of case studies is found in Davarian L. Baldwin, *In the shadow of the ivory tower: how universities are plundering our cities* (New York, Bold Type Books, 2021). Previous research on US universities as developers has usually focused on private elite institutions located in 'problem' urban areas, especially Columbia and New York University, but Baldwin's study shows that urban developer ambitions also shape public ordinary universities such as Arizona State University in Phoenix.

7 Mariana Valverde, Jacqui Briggs, Matt Montevirgen, and Grace Tran, "Public universities as real estate developers" *Studies in Political Economy*, vol. 101, no. 1, January 2020, 35–58.

established ones, for the most part) in regular co-working relationships with engineering and construction firms.[8] This may have advantages at the construction stage, insofar as the design will have been developed in close contact with the firms that are to build the asset. However, regular outsourcing of design means impoverishment of public-sector design capacity – and may also deprive the local elected authorities of significant input. The design will be brought to governing boards and maybe community meetings for 'consultation', but it is easy for designs to be protected from criticism by their sponsors, as they use various PR methods to shield specific choices from contestation, by invoking 'technical' factors that the unenlightened supposedly cannot grasp.[9]

A more ambitious type of 'deal' in the P3 repertoire is 'DBMO'. There, the private sector gets to design, build, maintain, and operate the infrastructure in question (which could be a public hospital or a prison, a bridge, or a transit line.) In such deals, operations meant to be outsourced are sometimes returned to the public authority in the jurisdiction – though this puts the public authority in the position of a mere contractor that can lose the contract. (That is one reason why the employment status of the staff – that is, whether they are public servants or not – is not as crucial a factor as public-sector labour unions believe.)

In some jurisdictions, it is not legal for governments to try to privatize the operation of certain services, especially policing and public transit (though workarounds can be found if the politicians ultimately in charge want to), but in others (in the UK and Australia especially), it is legally possible to outsource to the private sector work previously done, often on a monopoly basis, by a public-sector union. Some airport security jobs, for example, are now routinely performed by employees of private firms instead of by police or other public servants. The work of checking documents and questioning travellers, however, is unlikely to be privatized even

---

8 How private-sector entities join together to become private partners of a public entity is not a topic well covered in the large scholarly literature on P3s; with the agglomeration of the various corporations not being subject to freedom of information requests, investigative urban-beat journalists also focus exclusively on how risks and rewards are divided between 'the public' and 'the private'.

9 An example from my own research: when engaged in a participant-observation study of a Toronto housing P3 that took place before Regent Park (by which what was Donmount Court became Rivertowne), the community committee of which I was a member was told that the alleys in the new development could not be as narrow as the typical old-Toronto alleys found in the area because, we were told, the fire department needs a certain turning radius for its fire trucks. The architects had originally wanted to emulate or simulate the urban aesthetics of old Toronto, but nobody challenged the second-hand information about what fire trucks technically required.

in the most neoliberal deregulatory jurisdictions: control over the movement of people across frontiers has always been key to state sovereignty. But the key letter in the various P3 acronyms is one not included in DBMO – namely, F for 'financing'. It can be said, as a generalization that has exceptions, that consciously designed, purposively chosen 'branded' P3s (as opposed to the myriad de facto P3s that have existed for centuries) were invented in and by the Thatcher government. There the invention was known as the 'Private Finance Initiative'.[10] That technique was exported, among other routes in the brains and the briefcases of lawyers training in London in the Thatcher years, to other places. In the most populous province of Canada, Ontario, the British Private Finance Initiative (PFI) was the main source of ideas for the large special-purpose authority Infrastructure Ontario created in 2005. Its methods, along with the underlying belief in the inherent innovativeness and efficiency of the private sector promoted in the popular culture of the time, as well as among corporate elites, were also implemented in the significant province of British Columbia through the entity known as 'Partnerships BC', the infrastructure agency in charge of all major publicly commissioned projects. The techniques devised for and by the British Private Finance Initiative were also re-exported to other Canadian provinces, some of which, lacking experience in P3s and lacking extensive corporate law and consulting talent, contracted with either Infrastructure Ontario or Partnerships BC for larger privately financed projects.

Private financing is the key element of the diverse assemblages known as P3s. Other aspects of infrastructure work have been and will continue to be outsourced to architects, engineers, utility companies, and humble local firms doing sidewalk and road repairs. That does not necessarily weaken the public authority or reduce democracy if done transparently and rationally. However, private financing is more significant than other types of outsourcing from a governance and democracy point of view.

Private financing means that the private sector (a pension fund, a bank, a specialized infrastructure investor, such as Australia's Macquarie Bank) provides not only equity but also whatever debt is necessary to launch a project. They do it not out of public mindedness but for the sake of a future return. Importantly, governments everywhere hide the workings

10 See Mark Freedland, "Public law and private finance: putting the PFI in a public law frame" *Public Law*, 1998, 288–307. Private financing does not necessarily imply the financialization of public assets – financialization of public revenue streams and public assets is its own assemblage. An overview of financialization in the city context is provided in a special issue of the venerable journal *Urban Studies*, vol. 53, no. 7, 2016.

of private finance by frequently stating that 'the private sector will FUND such and such', statements which confuse the very important differences between funding and financing. The private sector does not fund public works and cannot be expected to do so. The private sector, including public-sector pension funds (which act just like the private money entities they legally are[11]) only **invests** in a project for the sake of a return that has to be larger than what can be got through passive investments.

Governments love private financing because it adds little or nothing to the government's debt load, in the short run. The traditional way of funding public works was for the government itself, or special purpose agencies (such as urban development corporations) to issue bonds or otherwise borrow to build something new. With private financing, the investors will insist on a rate of return that is better than what could be got by just sitting on their capital or lending it to governments.

One important detail is that in many cases, the principal is only payable at the end of the contract – 30 or 40 years being the standard time frame. Along the way, the private investor gets paid interest only. The consortium of various private-sector entities usually gets large lump sums at points such as 'substantial completion', but the financiers, usually located at a considerable distance from the project, work on a different temporality. The fact that private financing is not like a mortgage, where the borrower has to repay some of the principal along with interest all along, would make private financing of this type highly inconvenient for individuals since they are unlikely to be able to save up a large sum reserved for repaying the principal after 40 years. But for governments, putting off repaying the principal (that is, adopting the financial form known in the US as a 'bullet bond') is a benefit. A government can announce a multi-billion investment during an election campaign with the knowledge that the principal, put up by the large global funds that need secure places to park their billions long term, will only be due in 40 years – at which time perhaps inflation will have lowered the effective amount due, or, more certainly, the politicians in question will be either dead or out of office.

The difference between the temporality of ordinary consumer loans including mortgages and that of most infrastructure private financing is important. And the temporalities of lending and financing are rarely

---

11 On the governance of public-sector pension funds, major players in the infrastructure world, see a collection edited by Kevin Skerrett, Johanna Weststar and Simon Archer, *The contradictions of pension fund capitalism* (Urbana, IL, Labor and Employment Relations Association, 2017).

if ever justified with arguments. When going through dozens of Infrastructure Ontario contracts (contracts posted online, though with the financials redacted) in the early days of my P3 research, around 2013–15, I noticed that the term of the contract was almost always 40 years. Initially, I naively thought this meant the infrastructure itself was meant to last only 40 years – but then realized that bridges and roads last much longer. Not yet familiar with the financial industry, I puzzled over this, until an acquaintance in the pension fund business suggested to me that the temporality of infrastructure contracts has nothing to do with the material durability of the asset. The reason why pension funds love to finance infrastructure as an investment, my acquaintance suggested, is that pension funds are unusual players in the financial universe because they need to secure income over a very long period. The temporality of contracts is not discussed in any of the mountains of government documents I have consulted – time frames for 'financial closing' and for repaying the lenders are presented without explanation. But it is very plausible that the temporality of each type of institution's risk portfolio[12] should account for the marked difference between the length of the physical life of an asset and that of its legal existence.

Here it is useful to recall the discussion in Chapter 2 of the nineteenth-century British middle- and upper-class preference for 'consols', that is, government bonds that would generate revenue on a fixed schedule set in advance. The financing of public infrastructure by private entities such as pension funds and banks has a different logic. The government that ultimately will have to repay the billions in financing can always raise taxes – a key reason for the generally good credit rating of governments in wealthy countries – and thus increase, from one month to the next, its ability to make loan payments as required. But if it becomes necessary to raise taxes to repay the principal in 40 years, a whole new generation of politicians will be blamed, not the original decision-makers.

It is small wonder that investing in infrastructure has come to be seen as especially lucrative – but also especially appealing to funds interested in the very long term. Pension funds always invest in stocks and bonds too, but infrastructure investing suits their particular needs especially well.

---

12 An excellent account of the way in which contemporary finance has switched from investing in corporations to investing in portfolios diversified not in terms of any use value but purely in terms of higher vs. lower risk is Ivan Ascher, *Portfolio society: on the capitalist mode of prediction* (New York, Zone Books, 2016).

A useful overview of the issues plaguing large infrastructure project governance is found in the 2010 *International Handbook of Public-Private Partnerships*.[13] This collection restricts its scope to long-term infrastructure projects (PPPs in health-care delivery, in education, in research, and other fields have their own literatures). The book, featuring many of the key scholarly researchers in the area, shows that all manner of heterogeneous financial, construction, procurement, and legal arrangements can be found if one looks under the hood of either particular projects or a single government's norms and practices governing long-term infrastructure contracts. The introduction adds, usefully, that PPPs have no particular theory and did not arise from research. Rather, the term grew out of a more or less Thatcherite 'commonsense' notion that the private sector could do many things or even all things more efficiently than the public sector, and that over and above traditional contracts with construction and engineering companies, governments ought to be valuing private-sector expertise at all stages (including project evaluations and audits of infrastructure agencies, a field fraught with self-dealing, as mentioned in Chapter 1).

The handbook on P3s mentions, as a preliminary remark, that P3s may have been a recent invention as a term of art, but that, in fact, various forms of P3s have long existed. American cities, notably, have for at least a century devised creative assemblages of legal and financial tools that allow municipal governments to foster and encourage private-sector development, especially in forlorn downtown areas. While these governing innovations did not have a specific public-private moniker for a long time, histories of downtown redevelopment by US scholars reveal the taken-for-grantedness of public-private collaborations. In the 1950s, the norm was that the public sector provided land either free or at low cost, plus generous tax incentives meant to lure the private sector to build factories. Later the collaborations came to focus on revitalizing waterfronts, as a way to bring people, both tourists and suburbanites, back to downtowns largely abandoned by white middle-class people in the era of the suburban shopping mall. Such redevelopment projects required political and legal changes – such as the designation of a particular area as 'blighted' (in the 1930s–50s), as 'in need of improvement' (in the 1980s–90s), or as fitting some other

---

13 Graeme Hodge, Carsten Greve and Anthony Boardman, eds., *International handbook of public-private partnerships* (Cheltenham, Elgar, 2010).

category designed to funnel public benefits to a small area.[14] In general, a special district targeted for redevelopment (in the UK 'regeneration') often required what one could charitably call legal creativity – such as the 'Tax Increment Financing' that is now widespread across the US, which in theory finances future development using future business tax revenue in a particular area.[15]

Administrative law scholars have led the way in raising important questions about arrangements where public works are created and/or maintained not through regular contracts for particular services but through more complex arrangements that erode the accountability of public procurement processes. Graeme Hodge in Australia, Mark Freedman in the UK, and Ellen Dannin and Jo Freeman in the US, to name a few of the relevant scholars, have pointed out the potential – and sometimes the actual – pitfalls of planning public works by means not only of contracts with corporations (those contracts are as old as cities themselves) but by structuring the project as a separate entity, a 'partnership' that is not a partnership in the corporate law sense of the word but that distributes risks and responsibilities in specific ways, usually by means of private-law tools. To that extent public lawyers have on occasion complained more generally about "planning by contract" and "government by contract".[16]

The cry by public-minded administrative lawyers to be wary of "government by contract" and of the resulting "crumbling democracy"

14 One highly detailed study of one recent redevelopment project is Lynne Sagalyn's, *Power at ground zero: politics, money, and the remaking of Lower Manhattan* (New York, Oxford University Press, 2016). Sagalyn, a planning professor, previously undertook a detailed study of the Times Square redevelopment. In both case studies, much information is provided about the novel legal tools devised to carry out projects, though no general conclusion about legal innovation is provided. Similarly, Susan Fainstein's justly famous book *The city builders: property development in New York and London, 1980–2000* (Lawrence, KS, Kansas University Press, second edition, 2001) also contains much information about legal and financial techniques used or invented, but that too does not analyze the significance of the legal innovations.

15 See, for example, Bernard Frieden and Lynne Sagalyn, *Downtown Inc: how America rebuilds cities* (Cambridge, MA, MIT Press, 1997). Suburban 'tracts' of single-family detached houses also benefited from special benefits that only a public government could confer, but by contrast with downtown redevelopments, past and continuing government support for suburban tracts is rarely seen as part of the story of P3s. For one overview of the de facto P3s operative in suburban America, see Dolores Hayden, *Building suburbia: green fields and urban growth, 1820–2000* (New York, Vintage, 2003).

16 Jo Freeman and Martha Minow, eds., *Government by contract? Outsourcing and American democracy* (Cambridge, MA, Harvard University Press, 2009), and Ellen Dannin, "Crumbling infrastructure, crumbling democracy: infrastructure privatization contracts and their effects on local governance" (Penn State Law research paper no. 14–2011, 2011).

is certainly worth heeding. However, these critics often assume that re-nationalizing both actual infrastructures and the decision-making process is the remedy. Without falling into cliches about the supposed public-sector evils of corruption and inefficiency, one can nevertheless question whether moving decisions and asset ownership from the private sector to the public sector is feasible or even desirable as an all-purpose remedy. In some cases, renationalization of both structures and processes is clearly a good option, but in some cases, including most of the US, there was never a golden age of publicly owned efficient infrastructure to which current leaders could return.

As a matter of fact, private ownership has been the default setting in so many infrastructural fields that the feasibility of nationalization is very much in doubt. For example, the nationalization of Internet service providers is not something that even left-wing political parties are calling for, to my knowledge. Instead, the calls articulated now by both citizen groups and some government actors are for stricter government regulation of that private sector, one that has become virtually a necessity for both households and businesses. Along similar lines, the fact that natural gas companies are largely privately owned is not necessarily a problem; the problems, especially in regard to equity, become acute when prices and the quality of services are not regulated or not sufficiently regulated.

In this regard, it may be more useful to stop speaking not only about PPPs in general (a phrase that as I hope I have shown is deeply fraught with ambiguity and vagueness) but even about infrastructure. It may be that communications (telephone cables, fibre-optic cables, and all the computers that support those networks) that have since the beginning or for a long time been in private hands may be adequately regulated by a public authority (such as a utility commission) that has ready access to expert knowledge to evaluate corporations' calls for higher prices. Other types of infrastructure, from public transit to sewers and piped drinking water, could also benefit from being regulated by specific bodies if municipalization or nationalization is not feasible. This is not to undermine progressive calls for an expanded role for the public sector but simply to point out that continuing to rehearse the epic battle of 'public vs. private', a battle of abstract titans, has not proven very helpful.

In conclusion, we have seen that the term 'public-private partnership' (1) does not designate a specific thing or arrangement but functions rather as an umbrella term for a multitude of arrangements; (2) that insofar as P3s exist, they are not an invention of neoliberalism, having existed de facto for centuries; and (3) that deciding on the appropriate combination of resources and jurisdictions/authorities is likely best done at the local level rather than through a top-down one-size-fits-all template, whether that be nationalization or privatization.

Today's infrastructure agencies claim to be nimble and innovative because they use personnel and techniques from the private sector, but these agencies often turn into a micromanaging bureaucracy rather than acting as a stimulus to public-sector innovation. Studying how partnerships are actually put together, and with what effects, requires empirical research of particular situations since only that kind of research can identify when 'innovation' is only a rhetorical tool.

Within the common-law world, the standardization and regulation of PPPs are usually carried out by special-purpose bodies or agencies. In Latin America, by contrast, where one-off purely local legal assemblages are difficult to create and easy to challenge under expansive constitutional rights jurisprudence, national governments (in Argentina and Brazil, for instance) have passed national laws regulating PPPs – a measure that is not likely to be very effective insofar as (as has been shown in this chapter) both public and private actors can evade the new laws by labelling their arrangements as something different or unique.

Citizens interested in holding infrastructure actors accountable, therefore, need to familiarize themselves with the details of proposals and try to obtain the information that the actors in question are least likely to make readily available: financing details. Abstract generalities about the inherent virtues of either the public sector or of public law over private law will not be of much help in this search for increased levels of democratic participation.

Chapter 8

Smart cities

The word 'infrastructure' has in the past been used to talk almost exclusively about physical assets and networks: roads and bridges, electricity grids, sewage systems, and the like. However, Internet access has become almost a necessity for numerous activities. Arguments are now being put forward about the growing need to consider the 'tubes'[1] carrying digital signals not only as an infrastructure but a necessary infrastructure, something that ought to be provided as of right. The UN has developed norms about 'social and economic rights', norms that certainly don't have the force of law in most places but carry considerable political and symbolic weight, and are occasionally rendered effective in domestic legislation: the notion that there is a human right to housing, for example, has gained traction in many places.

Similarly, while in its early stages Internet access was a luxury enjoyed by small groups (composed almost completely of American men), nowadays Internet access, at least on a temporary basis, has become a necessity. Developments during the pandemic, such as the widespread adoption of online schooling and the expectation that in jurisdictions where 'vaccine passports' are being implemented everyone will store the relevant digital image on a 'smartphone', have accelerated this process. Hence, today there are calls for governments to at least help to provide affordable or free Internet access, even in remote and rural areas where such service is not profitable for commercial Internet service providers.[2]

---

1 The physicality of 'the Internet' is well documented in a popular-science book by Andrew Blum, *Tubes: a journey to the centre of the internet* (Harmondsworth, Penguin, 2013). The book does not make an explicit argument about the need to include Internet access in discussions about infrastructure planning, but it implicitly supports such an argument. A 54-minute free video of Andrew Blum speaking about the book is on YouTube.
2 In Canada, a northern country with large areas with small, scattered populations, the issue has not yet emerged as a national priority but has received attention – see

DOI: 10.4324/9781003254973-9

Aside from the emergence of campaigns to have Internet access be considered a right, other aspects of the politics of the digital world bear on infrastructure: for instance, the embedding of electronic surveillance in objects such as 'smart fridges' and 'smart home security systems', which could be the subject of a whole other book. But in a short book such as this, it is not possible to discuss all the topics that bear on the important question of how power is exercised through data collection. Instead, this chapter will focus on 'smart cities' – a very popular term, perhaps even a fad, that raises all the issues about infrastructure, regulation, and law in a context where the digital and the physical/material are necessarily intertwined. Let us begin with the problem of defining 'smart cities'.

What is a smart city anyway?

The term 'smart city' is often used without any definition, as if there is agreement about what might make one city 'smart' and another one not so smart. Even when a definition is given, the meaning is often extremely vague. When city managers talk with one another about their city's ambition to earn the label of 'smart', the definitions that circulate tend to assume that the serious crises faced by urban communities everywhere, from climate change to social inequality, can and should be addressed by collecting and analyzing vast amounts of data. The purpose of the data gathering and data analysis is often left unspecified but the implication is that data is the necessary fuel for what are always called 'solutions' – a word that circumvents the difficult political issue of who exactly has identified the problems for which flows of data will help to provide solutions.

Every person and every institution would like to think of itself as 'smart'. But 'smart city' talk reduces smartness not only to technological sophistication but more narrowly to sophistication in computing hardware and software. Apps are particularly popular in the 'smart city' space. The assumption behind the constant flow of PR for this or that new app is that with innovative user-friendly apps both city managers and citizens will become 'smart', as gadgets and sensors that are connected to each other via the Internet generate 'solutions' by consuming plenty of city-generated or crowd-sourced data.

It is of course true that modern computers, and data geeks to programme them and use them, are desirable for any city, and indeed for

---

Mariana Valverde and Alexandra Flynn, eds., *Smart cities in Canada: digital dreams, corporate designs* (Toronto, ON, Lorimer, 2020), especially Flynn's chapter on Nunavut.

any institution. It is important for critics of what one can call 'smart city ideology'[3] to not fall into simplistic denunciations of computers or of data gathering, and the same goes for critics of 'surveillance capitalism'. Not all data gathering is nefarious surveillance, and software engineers and data scientists can make an important contribution to today's many urban crises, including infrastructure crises. However, it is important to be sceptical about the presumed links between digital sophistication on the one hand and civic virtue on the other. Smart city promoters highlight the need to integrate social and cultural factors into the process of achieving 'smart city' status, but it is impossible to find, in practitioner discourses, good analyses of the gap between technical superiority and human happiness. In one particularly over-ambitious definition, smart cities are said to be those that promote 'liveability' – as if that quality, which differs a great deal from one neighbourhood to another and one group to another, never mind internationally, could be measured in a neutral technical manner.[4]

There is no accepted definition of a smart city, or even of a city seeking to be smart. It is therefore necessary to document what cities are doing as they pursue 'smartness' – which unfortunately often amounts to documenting what cities are purchasing from the tech sector to become smarter. As a general matter, cities have for many decades now generated vast troves of data, and not only in the global North. The reams of data, it must be emphasized, existed long before computerization. One city department will know exactly how many kilometres of paved streets or of water pipes there are; another will know exactly how many street lights have been erected and may know the average lifetime of the bulbs in the lights. Yet another department will know how many customers receive – or at least pay for – electricity if electric power has not been privatized. Another department will have a map of all the parks in the city, perhaps even including the

3 I have published articles, op-eds, and blog entries on smart city planning in a variety of venues, including planning and legal journals, but also more popular venues (such as the Centre for Free Expression's blog at Ryerson University). See Mariana Valverde and Alex Flynn, eds., *Smart cities in Canada: digital dreams, corporate designs* (Toronto, ON, Lorimer, 2020). The influential book by Harvard Business School professor Shoshana Zuboff, *The age of surveillance capitalism* (London, Profile Books, 2019), has greatly helped me to understand the political economy of smart cities, but I cannot share the classically humanist longing for individual autonomy that is the normative ground from which she elaborates her critique.

4 Mainstream 'smart city' talk can be found, for instance, on the website and the newsletters of the 'Smart Cities Connect' organization, an association of mid-size cities, mainly American. Both the tone/style and the content of that website are typical of the practitioner field.

location of each bench and each tree. And the local police will likely have ample information about how many tickets for illegal parking have been issued and perhaps also how many of those have been paid.

The production of data by and about cities is not new, even if up until recently most reams of data were found on paper documents rather than in electronic files.[5] However, cities being the poor cousins of the political system, the data sets were often inaccessible to all but a few managers, and by and large, especially in metropolitan centres, the data sets were not linked to one another. Nor could they be linked later since the troves of data, usually generated and kept at the level of department or agency, not of the city as a whole, were not formatted to allow for what computer folks call "interoperability".

Enter the tech industry. For several decades, tech companies (especially giants like IBM, Siemens, and Cisco but also many smaller, often local, start-ups) have been offering city managers, and indeed managers of public institutions generally, 'solutions' of various kinds. Almost invariably these so-called solutions were developed by computer and software experts, sometimes with the free labour provided by 'hackathons' – without prior study of what cities actually want and need. One company will offer 'smart' streetlights – which simply means lights that turn off automatically when natural light fails, regardless of clock time. Another will offer a 'smart' system for watering the greenery in parks. It is now common for parks departments, in the global North at any rate, to purchase sensors that detect humidity and automatically send a message, an electronic message, to a command centre that will turn on the sprinklers as needed. The sensors that are buried in the ground but are connected to the watering system may well help cities cut down on water bills, as well as cut down on labour costs, and they may keep new plants greener longer than the traditional person-powered watering methods, depending on staffing levels in parks. But whether this type of 'smart' system brings about a significant improvement in citizen enjoyment of parks is an open question. It is not only the ghost of Jane Jacobs who would say that having gardeners with hoses or watering cans makes a park more 'liveable' than one where automation has been instituted.

Like every other 'smart' innovation or gadget that I have read about or seen, the innovation consisting of humidity sensors and their physical

5 Even if computers are made available to city staff, the paper original may retain privileged status due to the fact that authentication and verification are more easily done on paper than online: Matthew Hull, *Government of paper: the materiality of bureaucracy in urban Pakistan* (Berkeley, CA, University of California Press, 2012).

and digital connection to the sprinklers and hoses does indeed serve a purpose: it is to that extent a 'solution'. But the point that engaged citizens ought to make in the many 'consultations' regarding smart city policies that are being held around the world is that cities may have other much more pressing problems, from the citizen point of view – such as a systematic maldistribution of park space, a distribution that usually matches the map of socio-economic difference within and among cities. To put it differently: if there are nice green parks in bourgeois areas and hardly any greenery in poorer areas, as is common in the global North but especially true in the South, making park watering more efficient may exacerbate existing inequalities, with richer families gaining nicer and greener parks but the poor continuing to lack green space.

A point repeatedly made by critical scholars of 'smart cities' is that technology-dependent solutions, such as those offered by tech innovators to managers and (mainly in the form of apps) to citizens, will be implemented in a context that is likely to be quite unequal and unjust. In that context, the 'solutions' might increase inequality rather than mitigate it. One example drawn from a very widely used innovation associated with 'smart cities' will help to underline this point before we go on to venture a definition of 'smart cities' that suits socio-legal analysis. That example is the 'smart' transit card, such as London's Oyster card.

The 'smart' transit card, which silently gathers vast amounts of personal data on a distant 'cloud' – which is not any place in the lawless and frontierless sky but rather a set of servers located in a large, air-conditioned warehouse owned by a tech company, in North America (likely to be located in Oregon or Washington State). This type of electronic card has been widely adopted around the world, for good reasons. First, it saves labour costs: fewer employees are needed to sell tickets or ensure riders have a valid ticket.[6] This efficiency undermines customer service, however, since fewer employees will be available to answer questions and ensure safety in stations. Often, increasing use of CCTV cameras in transit systems (instead of embodied 'eyes on the street' and 'eyes on the platform') is cited as the counterweight to the loss of jobs – a counterweight in keeping with the tech-driven logic of 'smartness'. Transit users will be told that they are now safer thanks

---

6 Of course, citizens can outsmart the card system; in Toronto, there have been reports of thousands of adults using the cheaper child cards fraudulently. Apparently, the automatic card readers at station or vehicle entrances only check that the card is valid and still has sufficient funds but cannot check the size or age of the passenger. Human beings cannot infallibly determine age, but they can certainly spot notoriously fraudulent uses of child cards.

to CCTV. They will not be told that the lack of safety was caused by the transit agency in the first place by drastic cuts in the way in which transit systems are staffed.

Secondly, commercially valuable data sets are created as passengers buy and use the cards. There are usually privacy laws that in theory prevent the sale of personal data (name, financial information, time, and route of travel) to the private sector, but a scandal concerning the smart card imposed across the Greater Toronto Area emerged when it was discovered that the smart card maker, Presto (which is not responsible to the Toronto Transit Commission) was allowing police to access the travel data of specific customers without judicial authorization and may have been selling aggregate data to private-sector interests.

It is important that in many instances the smart card provider is a separate corporation, either fully private or otherwise legally independent from and therefore not accountable to the public transit authority. As we will shortly see, at present some of the smart city projects in India promoted through the Modi government's 100 smart cities mission' include such smart card systems; the cards that are presented as most innovative can be used for various purposes (such as renting a shared bike or paying for parking) besides transit travel – which makes the risks of data mining and data misuse far greater. Most jurisdictions have very weak data protection and data governance frameworks, however, and even where those are more robust, such as the EU, the legal framework consistently emphasizes individual privacy while leaving more or less anonymized aggregate data marketization ungoverned. Thus, it is important for civic leaders to become informed about data governance problems and ask tough questions of potential tech providers. In many instances, perhaps most of the time, the choice of which system to purchase appears to be left to the information technology (IT) specialists; IT managers are knowledgeable about technical features but not necessarily about data governance risks.

These brief examples of smart city innovations show that while the marketing of the products emphasizes technical features, there are legal and political and social questions that need to be asked and adequately answered, which may get swept under the rug as both politicians and public-sector IT managers are dazzled by tech industry lobbying campaigns.

But do these complications *mean* that it is not possible to outline a definition of 'smart city' that is not tech-centric? Definitions provided by the tech sector and IT managers may serve their particular interests, but from the point of view of citizenship, from a socio-legal point of view, the most useful definition I have found is one provided by the

Irish critical data scholar and urban expert Rob Kitchin. He states that a smart city is not a particular set of objects or a state of technological sophistication but rather a "series of decisions about digitization and computing taken in an urban context".[7]

Kitchin's definition fits with this book's approach, which is to emphasize the dynamics of infrastructure as a field of governance – rather than fetishize technical features as the engineering profession tends to do. His definition can help those trying to understand the dynamics of infrastructure planning and delivery – what we could call 'infrastructure in use', borrowing from Umberto Eco's distinction between the static structure of a language and the way in which language is deployed in real life (which in turn draws on Saussure's influential differentiation of 'langue', as a structure, and 'parole', speech).

Kitchin's definition, emphasizing decisions rather than gadgets, is in keeping with critical scholarship on 'tech and the law', which as a field of study highlights the political and social consequences of decisions presented to the public as technical choices. Just as a particular new highway might be planned by civil engineers without consideration of the potential social consequences of the route chosen (and the economic and social consequences of making it a toll highway rather than a free public good), so too a 'smart streetlight' or a 'smart transit card' might emerge victorious in a procurement process that only considers cost and technical efficiency but neglects social and political effects. Doing some research on my own university's procurement of educational software that was made compulsory in teaching even before the pandemic – software that provides course websites with features facilitating some pedagogic goals but blocking others – I came to the tentative conclusion[8] that decisions about which system to purchase seemed

---

7 Rob Kitchin, "The real-time city? Big data and urbanism" *Geojournal*, vol. 79, no. 1, 2014. See also his book *The data revolution: big data, open data, data infrastructures and their consequences* (London, SAGE, 2014), which usefully points out that 'big data' does not refer to the size of a data set but rather to data sets that are interoperable and are in motion, connected to other data and updated, corrected and utilized. A nation's census for a particular year has a ton of data but that is arguably not big data because (by law) the giant data set lacks mobility and interaction.

8 The conclusion remains tentative because in keeping with the institution's lack of transparency, both the content of the contracts signed with tech providers and the signatures on those contracts were not made available to me. A few years ago, a national Canadian organization initiated an access to information request for university contracts with Google and Microsoft; after two years, some of the contracts were released but with the details of interest redacted.

to be left to the IT specialists. Neither the university's own experts on digital inequities nor critical scholars of big data, inside or outside the university, were consulted and neither were student groups. Further, there is no way to opt out of the software; there is not even a token 'I accept' button to click since the university is the only customer.

Today, smart city consultants and lobbyists for tech firms claim that they include social factors such as equity in their proposals, but until the process of tech procurement, within municipal offices as well as in public institutions such as transit systems and universities, is made much more transparent than it currently is, it will be very difficult for civic-minded stakeholders to check whether equity is in fact a consideration. It will also be very difficult to present an alternative plan if the details of the existing contracts and arrangements remain shrouded in secrecy. Further, when a potential vendor or lobbyist is presenting a product to an audience such as city councillors (or university administrators), the audience is unlikely to have sufficient knowledge of how the gadget or app or large-scale 'urban operating system' is already being used elsewhere. Independent research is necessary to provide disinterested information to the people who have the authority to sign contracts. And in this regard, few decisions are as significant as those taken, often years in advance of any local 'smart city' innovations, in regard to the fundamental computing infrastructure to which particular features, gadgets, and apps are added: so-called urban operating systems.

The invisible infrastructure underpinning 'smart cities': operating systems

A rare empirical comparative empirical study of cities around the world that claim 'smartness' is the 2020 book by Andres Luque Ayala and Simon Marvin, *Urban Operating Systems: Producing the Computational City* (published by MIT Press in the US but available freely online). Covering Barcelona, Delhi, Dublin, New York, and Rio de Janeiro, and informed by the large body of previous work produced by the two authors and their collaborators, the fascinating study shows that even when city managers are happy to pursue the panopticon-style dream of a central control room for all flows of city data − not an easy feat, given that in most big cities departments and agencies operate with much autonomy − Big Brother fails to materialize. That happened to the early adopter of the central control room notion, Rio de Janeiro − one of the first customers for IBM's operating system, marketed until recently under the copyrighted brand 'smarter cities'.

Even in the optimistic, modernizing, and relatively prosperous years just before the Rio Olympics and the World Cup of football, the city of Rio did not manage to actually create a central place to which all data streams flow and that can indeed control the city (as the ambitious label 'central control room' suggests). The rapid decay of Brazil in general and Rio's mega-event-oriented infrastructure that has occurred since the study was conducted makes it very likely that Big Brother remains an unrealized goal.

Underlining the point that Big Brother failed to come to life despite IBM's interest in using Rio as a loss leader, the same book contains a fascinating chapter on a completely separate project undertaken by Google and the municipality of Rio, together. This was a project designed to 'put the favelas on the map', literally and symbolically, by sending favela inhabitants armed with GPS and fancy phones with lots of data around their neighbourhoods.

The favela-mapping exercise required locals to walk or climb up and down the steep inclines of Rio's favelas and undertake mapping in keeping with the Google Maps methods and formats. Many of the favelas do not have regular streets, and houses do not usually have numbers, so the work was laborious. If one were a tech optimist one would say this was a perfect public-private partnership: a progressive municipal administration wanted to facilitate economic activity in the favelas and grant the inhabitants the civic pride of being 'on the map', while Google, on its part, never turns down an opportunity to gather large amounts of new data. That Google's agenda was rather colonialist may have been apparent to the hard-working local youth who were sent on mapping exercises, but they may have thought that in the current neoliberal era communities can take advantage of a strange-bedfellows convergence of interests, since plenty of foreign tourists would want to have maps on their phones that made for 'authentic' urban experiences – and in Rio, that means bringing tourists to the favelas rather than to the wealthier areas near the beaches. PPPs or deals are often said to be 'win-win' situations just because there's a potential for both participants to gain something. The win-win language regularly used in municipal politics, as well as in business, however, conceals the fact that one side's gain may be much smaller or less financially valuable than the other side's.

The fact that most large cities, in the global South as well as the North, made early, often unpublicized decisions to buy a whole host of computing resources (including future time from technicians and maintenance personnel, as well as cables and machines) from one of the established big firms has set the scene for later, more publicly visible smart city innovations such as transit smart cards, 'smart' traffic lights, and the like. IBM, Cisco, Siemens, Hitachi, and a couple of other Chinese and European firms were selling 'urban operating systems' to city governments in places like Rio before there was much talk of smart city projects.

The contracts signed with these firms are not usually public. Indeed, even the technical architecture of these systems and their potential downstream consequences and limitations may not be fully known even by the local IT managers. And it's not clear what the word 'system' means, or perhaps conceals, in the context of the phrase 'urban operating systems'. I asked someone who used to design such systems for one of the US giants what exactly an urban operating system is, and his answer was 'some combination of hardware and software'. Clearly 'urban operating system' is an umbrella term more than a specific thing or set of things.

In many jurisdictions, most contracts signed by city departments (such as for road paving) are made public or are available to citizens through access to information processes. But the 'trade secret' category of intellectual property is unlikely to be invoked in ordinary contracts such as for road paving, whereas it is very likely to be invoked by tech companies competing with one another for patents, markets, and staff. This means not only that citizens cannot know what their tax dollars bought but also that managers and politicians in other jurisdictions will have difficulties gathering sufficient information to make informed choices. This is important since bad procurement decisions haunt the whole smart city space; the academic literature is full of examples of what one might call worst practices. If other cities' contracts are not shared either with the public or with other jurisdictions, it will be very difficult for the most conscientious of city actors to make informed decisions: the traditional 'jurisdictional scan' done by policy analysts will be very superficial, likely based only on the glowing self-interested reports produced by the tech sector and by the numerous consultants who work in the smart city space.

A local example of the 'vendor lock-in' problem that is inherent in the purchase of urban operating systems may help to concretize this point. During the pandemic, the Toronto city council began to allow virtual council meetings, including votes. With Toronto being a Cisco rather than an IBM city, the meetings had to be held using Cisco's Webex. Many councillors stated a preference for Zoom since like everyone else they were using that in their private lives and in their non-official meetings with constituents. But Cisco Webex had to be used for official council and council committee meetings, despite its increasingly obvious flaws. The numerous complaints councillors made proved fruitless. By the time the pandemic hit, it was too late to change the 'urban operating system'.

It is not known whether specific clauses in the contract prevented the city from seeking new vendors; often, it is the technical features of the old system more than contract clauses that prevent innovation and open competition. The 'urban operating system' is a hybrid where legal details (contract clauses) are only one element.

Linking apps to municipal bonds: the Indian government's '100 smart cities mission'

Like many other Indian cities, Bhubaneswar is known for both ancient Hindu temples and an educated workforce. It is also known for frequent seasonal flooding. The risk of flooding could be mitigated with some of the 'smart' alert systems that other cities have implemented (in South America for example, where alerts for impending mudslides and floods exist in many cities). But flooding was not part of the picture in Bhubaneswar's smart city proposal, ranked number one in the government's competition, which began shortly after the 2015 election of President Narendra Modi.[9]

As was demanded by the government of India in its call for proposals, the Bhubaneswar plan was not elaborated by locals – who might have prioritized the flood risks, perhaps – but rather by an international consulting firm with headquarters in Toronto, IBI. (Other well-ranked proposals were written and formatted, with plenty of full-colour illustrations, by global consulting firms such as McKinsey.)

The Bhubaneswar proposal jumped scales, as geographers say, and achieved international fame when in 2017 it won the prize for 'best smart city plan' from the American Planning Association – a reputable organization led by university professors of planning, not self-interested corporations.

As is the case with smart city plans everywhere, in the global South and in the North, the proposal written for Bhubaneswar, by the consultants but with input from state and local officials, claimed to include what smart city planners usually call 'citizen engagement' – a vague

9 For an excellent account of the Indian smart city program, see Ayona Datta, "The digital turn in postcolonial urbanism" *Transactions of the Royal Geographical Society*, 2018.

word that does not necessarily indicate either accountability or significant participation. The 56,000 Facebook likes that a draft of the proposal garnered when it was made public were counted as if 56,000 citizens had been meaningfully consulted – and this in a country where less than half of the population has Internet access.

But 'social inclusion' and equity talk are standard features of smart city plans (if not of smart city realities). Accordingly, the Bhubaneswar plan promised to address the safety needs of women and children and the housing needs of low-income temporary migrant workers. In regard to safety, domestic violence or gender injustice are not mentioned; safety is imagined as flowing inevitably from the CCTV cameras installed in the central city's public spaces. There are photos of such cameras; one cannot tell how many there are or how the images captured are used, but some at least do exist. By contrast, the 'slum-dwellers' and migrant workers said to need housing appear to still be, years later, waiting for the housing to commence. (Slum clearances have been documented in other smart cities around India, but it is not clear to what extent such 'clearances' would have taken place regardless of smart city status).

One notable feature of the Bhubaneswar plan that has been implemented is the Odyssey smart card. This appears to be what in the tech sector is called a digital wallet since it is meant to be used not only for transit fares but also for paying parking tickets and, probably most importantly, for paying one's municipal utility bills.[10]

The fact that the Odyssey card exists – although data on how many people use it is not available, and one ought never to overestimate the actual adoption of new apps and gadgets – while the new housing remains unbuilt is not an accident. Here we have to return to the theme of municipal finance already canvassed in Chapters 2 and 4. The government of India's website for the 100 smart cities mission has a tab labelled 'financing'. Clicking on that brings one to a slide deck; the first few slides do not provide facts but rather complaints – complaints from the national level about the fact that Indian municipalities are very slow and inefficient in collecting fees and charges due to them.

---

10 Digital wallets may be the most popular smart city fad of 2021. In early summer 2021, Toronto city council approved, with some dissent, a contract with an American digital wallet provider, PayIt. That the PayIt system would necessarily contain many different types of data, from property ownership to car ownership to water and electricity usage, and that such 'big data' contains inherent data mining and privacy risks, did not seem to deter either the mayor or the officials – from a business-oriented 'partnerships' department – who promoted the contract.

In 2018, global consultant McKinsey praised (in a paper no longer available on their website) the Indian government's push to have municipalities improve their credit rating so they could begin to play in international municipal bond markets. Local research groups and scholars such as Ayona Datta have pointed to the role of the smart cities mission in promoting, perhaps unrealistically, municipal financial autonomy – so as to decrease the transfer payments from higher levels that have traditionally kept all but the wealthiest and largest Indian municipalities dependent on the central state.

In keeping with this ideal of municipal financial autonomy, the Indian government imposed a governance condition on all smart city proposals: to sidestep the elected municipal council in favour of a new entity created to develop and implement (and evaluate, they said!) each smart city plan – an entity constituted legally as a special purpose vehicle (SPV). As mentioned in earlier chapters, the SPV form has been used for some time to isolate infrastructure projects legally and financially so they can pursue financing independently of states or localities. In fact, SPV's have not (or not yet) been set up in many of the 100 chosen cities – but there is an SPV called "Bhubaneswar Smart City".

It is unclear whether the Modi government imagines that if some SPV's emerge as PPPs lacking the transparency and accountability of municipal governments, the quest to render Indian municipalities (outside of global Mumbai and Kolkatta) financially visible in private finance markets will be a good tool. Setting up a separate SPV may not in fact help boost the credit rating and hence the global financial possibilities of the relevant municipalities. The Port Authority of New York, a kind of SPV, was in excellent financial health while the city of New York languished in the 1960s and 1970s.

But whatever the success or failure of the project to boost municipalities' credit ratings, we see here how the Indian government's 100 smart cities mission seems to merge, at least in intentions and in chosen legal tools, with other features of neoliberal urbanism and neoliberal infrastructure planning and delivery. Besides imposing the SPV quasi-corporate, non-democratic form, the Indian government also required that cities that wanted to compete for the special funding needed to demonstrate that they had 'partnered' not only with the global proposal-writing consultants already mentioned but also with global tech vendors, such as IBM, Cisco, or Hitachi. Such a requirement is of course in conflict with the Indian government's stated goal of promoting a domestic high-tech economy, but it is well in keeping with the logic of global infrastructure planning.

Going forward it will be necessary for case studies of particular smart city plans/realities to be undertaken by India-based researchers. But the well-documented ambitions and desires of the Delhi-based promoters of smart city projects across India do tell a story of their own.[11] That story, along with the information about smart cities outside of India provided in the early part of the chapter, show that while computing innovations may dazzle people and create the impression that the digital is a world of its own, in fact, the network of modems, cell phone towers, computers, transatlantic cables, and electricity flows that plays such an important role in our present is not unique. Just as it has long been said that war is too important to be left to the generals, so too the complex issues around data and computing are too important to be left to IT specialists.

11 I acknowledge here the research done for me by Bethamehi Joy Siem and Shivanga Mishra at the National Law School in Bangalore. I also acknowledge the analyses of urban governance in India shared by Prasad Khonalkar.

Chapter 9

'Value for money' assessments

'Value for money' (routinely turned into the acronym VFM, a semantic move that gives the term an air of scientific or technical sophistication) is a term in ordinary speech; someone can say that 'I bought this car because it was good value for money', and the intended meaning will be readily apparent, especially if the car in question is less than brand new. In the rarefied world of infrastructure specialists, however, VFM is not in use among construction workers. Instead, it has been turned into a term of art at a higher level than the frontlines of construction, among those who make decisions and also those who obediently produce documents and data justifying the decisions. Spoiler alert: for the most part, the phrase is used to validate decisions taken for any number of disparate reasons to turn a public works project or even a whole government's infrastructure plan into a series of PPPs – a decision that is everywhere more political than technical.

And yet, the term VFM and the associated techniques of calculation and justification work in such a way as to make the decision to embrace the PPPs described in Chapter 7 and in other chapters look rational and not subject to political critique – rational in the sense of economic rationality. The phrase, as found in the infrastructure-enabling field, plays a role that is ideological in the strict Marxist sense of the word: it actually promotes particular economic interests while appearing to serve the general interest, the public interest.[1]

---

1 The term 'ideology' is often used extremely loosely to characterize any political program or set of values one doesn't like, but there is a more precise meaning first theorized by Karl Marx: the way in which the economic interests of the capitalist class are presented as if they served the general good – as in the American phrase 'what is good for General Motors is good for the country'. In the case of the infrastructure-enabling field, VFM is ideological precisely in Marx's meaning of the term. VFM assessments could of course be used in less

DOI: 10.4324/9781003254973-10

Ideally, a VFM calculation is a comparison of the costs and benefits of turning a public works project into a public-private partnership, with the comparison carried out in order to decide whether that mode (as described in Chapter 7) is appropriate for a project, or whether conventional public procurement and public finance are more appropriate. That sounds rational, technical, and politically neutral. But there is no such thing as political neutrality and fairness to all businesses in the world of infrastructure, as previous chapters have shown but as is particularly evident if one looks closely at the way in which VFM analyses are performed and utilized.

The Organization for Economic Co-operation and Development (OECD) and the World Bank are only two of the global organizations that have been promoting the use of VFM calculations. These global guardians of transparency and technical rationality are able to acknowledge, from their Olympian supra-state height, that the risk-pricing calculus that is at the heart of VFM calculations is often performed by public authorities (such as Ministries of Transportation or Infrastructure) that put a rather heavy thumb on the scales so as to favour the private sector and prevent innovation within public sectors.

In 2013, the World Bank held a workshop on VFM in their Washington, DC, headquarters, inviting infrastructure agencies from several jurisdictions – including Chile, notorious for rapid privatization of public works; the UK, also known for enthusiastic privatization, as well as for the invention of the 'Private Finance Initiative'; South Korea; India; South Africa; and the subnational jurisdictions of Virginia, USA, and British Columbia, Canada. The report from that workshop is written in anodyne understated bureaucratese, but a few points are made that suggest (if read carefully) that all is not well in the realm of public-private infrastructure partnerships.

One key finding – mentioned as if it were unimportant – is that the data about past projects that would be required to truly assess costs and benefits of private vs public financing and procurement of projects still at the planning stage do not exist: "few governments systematically carry out ex post VFM assessments of P3 projects".[2] In Canada, the largest infrastructure agency, Infrastructure Ontario, does not carry out project

---

ideological ways – for instance, to decide among different ways of providing for community needs – but in the infrastructure field, it is routinely used to make it seem that private financing and procurement are better for the public than conventional public-sector methods.

2 World Bank, *Value-for-money analyses: practices and challenges* (Washington, DC, World Bank, 2013).

evaluations; Partnerships BC says it does, but these amount to longer than average press releases and are full of photos of smiling public-sector workers but very short on anything resembling an objective analysis. The general lack of project evaluations is a systematic flaw that makes any VFM calculation far more subjective and arbitrary than it needs to be. To give a homey analogy: if I didn't know how much people have been paying for homes similar to the one I want to buy, I would not be in a good position to decide if the house the eager agent is showing me is indeed VFM.

In a world where audits and key performance indicators hover over every activity, public or private, it is indeed remarkable that so few governments bother to collect data on past projects in order to ensure that future decisions are evidence-based. And when the World Bank politely says, "few governments", the reader of such documents will know that they mean 'negligible to zero'. Further, even when the effort is made to perform technical rationality by undertaking a VFM ahead of making the choice whether to use public or private procurement and financing, many governments appear to believe that a single VFM can be recycled, as a 'test case', for other projects that may have significant differences. The lack of interest in project evaluations and the absence of careful comparisons of costs and benefits carried out by independent experts are closely linked to the fact that PPPs have been a hot political topic for decades now, with public-sector unions and social democratic parties routinely opposing them on principle and conservative parties and the private sector favouring them, also on principle. When people come to an issue with their minds made up in advance, facts do not matter a great deal.

Governments that led the privatization push of the early neoliberal era – Chile and the UK being major leaders – seem to have recently curbed their enthusiasm to some extent. Perhaps under pressure from the progressive government of Michelle Bachelet, Chile performs its infrastructure VFM calculations in a way that appears fair, comparing what private financing will ultimately cost the public purse to what government would have to pay to borrow the funds (by issuing government bonds or borrowing from global banks). Thumbs are not put on the 'private' side of the scale, in other words (or at least that was the case in 2013). By contrast, "most governments" (including British Columbia and Ontario) adjust the calculation by including a figure (unjustified by any actual data) for the price of the risks that the government is supposedly transferring to the private sector.[3] Thus, what

---

3 Despite a stinging 2014 report on the inadequacy of VFM calculations for large infrastructure projects delivered by the auditor-general of Ontario, Infrastructure Ontario tipped the

is called the PSC (the Public-Sector Comparator) is made to appear more expensive than the private finance option, by the simple method of adding a purely hypothetical cost to the public side, a figure based on insiders' guesses about the price of the transferred risks.

In the UK, the original home of the Private Finance Initiative that launched a thousand P3 ships, the VFM calculation has been improved since its early days. The key factor here is that the calculation (such as it is) has been moved from the final to the early stages of decision-making – a temporal move that clearly makes it possible to say that VFM is indeed helping to guide decisions rather than what even the World Bank report calls a practice "to rationalize an earlier decision".[4] And the current bible for both national and local authorities wanting to propose infrastructure projects, the British "Green Book", now requires public authorities to consider three different options for finance and procurement, including 'business as usual' – a methodology that may well result in the choice to use conventional public procurement.[5]

The political winds have moved on in both Chile and the UK since 2013, so the World Bank report has to be taken with a grain of salt. But it is interesting that the most enthusiastic evangelists of both outright privatization and private financing modified their methodology.[6] And in the UK, the reform appears to have survived into the Boris Johnson era. One useful reform is that government guidance documents in the infrastructure field now recognize that some risks (such as what they call "landscape" and "historic" [sic]) are not quantifiable. Whether efforts are supposed to be made by British local authorities and infrastructure providers to somehow measure and count risks to these non-monetary goods is unclear; economists after all claim that

---

scales even more towards the private sector in 2015 (as though thumbing their nose at the auditor-general) by adding an "innovation factor" – a purely hypothetical number used to quantify the purported benefits of construction 'innovation', assumed to be possible only in the private sector. See Infrastructure Ontario, *Assessing VFM* (2015 report, by none other than Deloitte, a consultant heavily implicated in the Canadian P3 infrastructure field).

4 World Bank, *op. cit.*, 20.

5 *The Green Book: Central government guidance on appraisal and evaluation* (London, HM Treasury, 2018).

6 Scholars working within the 'audit society' framework discussed in Chapter 1 would note that what the UK has done by way of curbing the ideological enthusiasm for the private sector is not stop putting its thumb on the scales but instead adding more layers of 'quality assurance' – that is, audit. An example of the proliferation of what Michael Power called "rituals of verification" is the Department of Transport's report unironically called *Strength in numbers: the DfT analytical assurance framework* (first issued 2014, updated May 2021).

they can monetize everything from the financial value of traffic congestion to the "value of a prevented fatality"[7]

Newcomers to the principles and practices of the Private Finance Initiative appear to be less wary, as is often the case with new converts. Even the World Bank 2013 workshop participants, all government enablers of PPPs, were in agreement that the quantitative VFM analysis that has been disseminated as the key method to justify PPPs gives the appearance of having mathematically proved that such partnerships are best when, as the practitioners in question all admitted, the use of numbers (especially dollar amounts ascribed to future imponderable risks) is highly misleading given the major assumptions that underlie the quantification exercise.

A case study: Infrastructure Ontario's VFM methodology

Drawing on what has already been explained in Chapter 7 about PPPs, it is possible to describe the ideological work of VFM quite succinctly. Since 'inscription practices' from the realm of free-market economics are taken for granted as suitable for decision-making (or decision-justifying) concerning infrastructure projects and since the supposedly neutral professionals who are actually charged with doing VFM calculations are all part of the same public-private infrastructure-enabling field (dominated by a small number of very large firms including global consulting agencies), numbers will indeed be produced, but whether the figures are evidence-based is a whole other question. The fact that as the World Bank 2013 report notes, in many jurisdictions, VFM's are only done **after** a decision has already been taken to undertake a project as a P3, is surely telling. That gives the VFM analysis the same kind of bias documented among police detectives who only send forensic evidence for testing that is associated with the person they already think has done the crime.

But it is worthwhile, from the point of view of citizen engagement with the fiscally and environmentally very significant world of infrastructure planning, to get into the weeds of the VFM exercise. We will do so here using a case study I conducted a few years ago but which is still highly relevant since the public authority in question (Infrastructure Ontario) has only slightly changed its methods, and unlike in the UK the small changes have only tipped the balance even further to favour private-sector power.

7 *Green book, op. cit.,* 62.

PPPs are routinely justified – or 'explained' in what amount to propaganda – as a great innovation in infrastructure planning that serves to shift the notorious risks of delays and excess expenses to the private sector. The language used is always imprecise; the phrase routinely used is that a P3 contract 'assigns risks to the party that is best situated to assume them'. The phrase acts to remind citizens of all the boondoggles and serious delays that have been well publicized in public works in their own jurisdiction, as well as reminding the more fiscally conservative citizenry of the way in which infrastructure budgets that are approved balloon as time goes on.

Popular discontent with public-sector boondoggles is certainly justified in the global North as well as in the global South. However, two points should be made that are routinely hidden from public view by the public authorities who announce new projects. One concerns budgets. It is very difficult for infrastructure owners and providers to persuade politicians to commit large sums. Therefore, it has become routine to underbudget initially, knowing that once the project is under construction, it will be far easier to get approval for the necessary extra funds since few politicians want to be seen to be abandoning major public works halfway through. (In my own university, building budgets are routinely kept low during the approvals process, but balloon afterwards – and the amended proposal rarely has to return to the governing board for approval.)[8] In general, there is an inherent tendency in the public sector to knowingly underbudget. In addition, it is often more advantageous to public-sector entities to spread out costs over several fiscal years, especially if they are attempting to pay as they go, out of annual revenues, rather than borrow one large sum.

Those features of the public sector and its budgets are the reason why P3 proponents can boast that P3 projects come in "under budget", especially in very large projects where there are very few local firms that can feasibly undertake the construction. (In Toronto, for instance, two firms, Aecon and Ellis Don, undertake virtually all major construction projects, and in the province of Ontario, two engineering firms, the Montreal-based SNC Lavalin and the Spain-based Dragados, do most of the work for major transportation projects.) The budgets of major P3 infrastructure projects (the HS2 in the UK, for example) are astronomical from the start, which then means it is easier to stay within the budget. The VFM calculus, if one can call it that, is

---

8 This is based in part on Governing Council documents and in part on personal communication from a local architect with much experience.

key here since it routinely overestimates the price that the public sector would have had to pay for risks that are shifted to the private sector to make the P3 option look more attractive.

Another factor facilitating very generous initial budgets for P3 projects is that undertaking any major infrastructure project in any jurisdiction involves not only having or gaining approval from local politicians but also retaining political support until completion. Electoral politics poses a grave risk to any private partner (a recent example being the abandonment of a huge airport project that had already broken ground by Andres Manuel Lopez Obrador as he became president of Mexico). As private law tools, contracts remain valid even during political upheavals, but cancellation payments do not always suffice to compensate the private-sector firms involved. Thus, the private sector has a great incentive to overbudget initially; their ability to extract additional payments along the way, as public entities routinely do, is highly variable since infrastructure projects are inherently very political.

In keeping with this differentiated logic, Infrastructure Ontario, whose major projects are all P3s, regularly overbudgets – which is easy since projects worth $200 million or $500 million, never mind several billion, are not the sort of thing that citizens or politicians could independently price. The VFM hence plays a crucial role: the calculation of costs and benefits (which includes guesses about the what the price would be of assuming risks such as weather delays) shows that private financing and procurement is best, even though it is widely known that most governments have a better credit rating than private corporations and can thus borrow money themselves considerably cheaper.[9]

The visual representation of VFM calculations varies across jurisdictions. But in Ontario, as in many other situations, the VFM calculus is rendered in full colour as a set of two bar graphs, one labelled 'public procurement' or 'traditional procurement' and the other labelled 'P3' or some synonym. It is routine in the P3 world to justify the choice of P3 procurement and finance by comparing the preferred option to a hypothetical 'Public-Sector Comparator' (abbreviated as PSC, of course, to lend the exercise an air of technical expertise). The PSC is not generated by public authorities, however, or by using data from publicly procured and financed projects. It is generated by the P3 proponents themselves (often featuring consultants who write reports for the hand that continually feeds them), and it is based in part on realistic cost projections but also on purely hypothetical prices

9 Matti Siemyaticki and Naheed Farooqui, "Value for money and risk in public-private partnerships" *Journal of the American Planning Association*, vol. 78, no. 3, 2012, 286–99.

ascribed to the risks that the public sector would have incurred if they had not gone the P3 route. The bar graphs always show the private option as coming out cheaper. Eager citizens who look at the reports posted online for each project on the Infrastructure Ontario website can 'see with their own eyes' that P3s are the best option.

On top of that, in keeping with the British PFI and the general 'audit society' mania for layers of assurance and verification, each project file on the IO website contains a document that assures the public that the VFM was done properly. These are simple letters, often just one page, on the letterhead of one of the handful of global consulting firms that earn considerable income from their participation in P3s – namely, Ernst and Young, Deloitte, and KPMG. The numbers placed in each little box for the type of cost, including 'reserved risk' and 'shifted risk', do not come with footnotes or calculations; they are simply numbers. The unwary citizen might think that Ernst and Young or Deloitte or KPMG have actually audited Infrastructure Ontario since audits are what originally gave all three firms their start; it is how they became global giants. However, the unwary citizen would be wrong. The letters in question merely state that the VFM was performed "in accordance with Infrastructure Ontario's methodology".

Of course, the methodology is what needs to be scrutinized, not the arithmetic, as the auditor-general of Ontario pointed out in her 2014 report, and as even the insiders present at the World Bank in 2013 seemed to admit. But citizens today like to have striking full-colour visuals, such as the bar graphs of Infrastructure Ontario reports that purport to allow them to 'see for themselves' that private financing and procurement is indeed better and cheaper.

The final point in this mini-case study is that the scale at which infrastructure is made visible to citizens – the scale of the single 'deal' (see Chapter 5) used by Infrastructure Ontario is typical of infrastructure agencies, and the choice of scale for reporting has notable effects on democracy. Websites belonging to Partnerships BC and the Australian infrastructure agency are replete with brief descriptions of ongoing and future projects, often featuring full-colour drawings or photos (Infrastructure Ontario is more text-heavy). As legal geography scholars have shown, and as has been documented in the chapter on 'the deal', the one-project-at-a-time scale may make a particular project visible to the public – although whether what is actually shown facilitates democratic engagement or hinders it is an open question – but what it hides from view, necessarily, are the prior decisions about which project to select out of the many possible and desirable ones that could be pursued in any one jurisdiction. That decision was made at another scale, another level, in rooms or in phone meetings different from those where the photos and reports are produced.

Conclusion

For those readers whose eyes tend to glaze over when presented with a set of numbers (and unfortunately the legal and socio-legal worlds are rather full of people like that, including the present author), it may seem tedious and unnecessary to delve into such practices as the VFM assessments. However, as Wendy Espeland and other sociologists and historians of quantification have shown, numbers play today a very important role in justifying a whole range of political projects, progressive and otherwise. And to help shed light on what governing work is being done by numbers or under the banner of numbers, we do not usually need to understand calculus or know how to do statistical regressions. The numbers that are relevant politically are usually what one could call 'bare' numbers – just numbers, without the calculations that generated them (if there were indeed calculations). And numbers have considerable mobility. Numbers that may have once been produced by experts in a highly technical context can suddenly begin circulating in different, novel networks, and can play unexpected political and social, and even legal roles. (The number of daily COVID-19 cases, for example, has multiple uses.)

We who preferred the humanities and/or the anti-quantitative ethos of law to secondary school mathematics ought to question our knee-jerk response to charts or even plain numbers. In many cases, the governing work the numbers do can become readily apparent to critical socio-legal scholars – perhaps more easily than to the 'technical' folks who might have produced them in the first place. Just as we have taken it upon ourselves to educate the larger public about the unexpected ways in which phrases such as 'human rights' and 'property rights' are or can be used, so too, if we overcome our fear of numbers, we can help educate the citizenry about what familiar numbers circulating in the public sphere show and don't show.[10] It is not a coincidence that the British Department of Transport chose the title "Strength in Numbers" for its detailed guide on how to measure risks and count costs in planned projects. We too can exercise our critical faculties in respect of numbers, as well as of legal or quasi-legal phrases and texts.

10 See Fernando Tamayo Arboleda and Mariana Valverde, "The travels of a set of numbers: the multiple networks enabled by the Colombian 'estrato' system" Social and Legal Studies vol. 30 no. 5, 2021, 685–703.

Chapter 10

Conclusion

Mainstream thinking about law portrays law as acting on the world from outside and/or from above to regulate conflicts, punish crimes, and generally bring order to an unruly world. Much of the legal profession and the legal academy also take this view, implicitly. For example, administrative lawyers frequently deplore the ways in which state officials use and misuse their discretion and suggest stronger laws and regulations be created to rein in the discretion that is inherent to interpreting and applying the law. This view of law as acting from above also lies at the core of criminal law and criminal procedure: both defense lawyers and law professors see stronger legal constraints as the main solution to problems such as police racial profiling.

The view that law is a superstructure that regulates social, economic, cultural, and political relations in the service of fairness, nondiscrimination, transparency, accountability, and even democracy is not confined to legal circles. Media accounts of such issues as state violence against marginalized groups also often suggest that if domestic law proves insufficient, international criminal law should be used to punish and hence indirectly to prevent acts of violence against collectives. Meanwhile, feminist activists have for many years attempted, and sometimes succeeded, in reforming the laws governing sexual assault and domestic violence in the assumption that better laws will minimize gender-based harms.

But this commonsense view has been challenged for many years now. The 'law and society' movement that from the 1960s onward revolutionized the legal academy held as one of its founding insights that far from acting from above, the law can be shown to **constitute** the realms of human conduct that it then tries to regulate. 'Society', 'the economy', 'culture', 'the state', 'the family', and 'the corporation' have been shown to be in large part constituted through legal mechanisms and legal thinking.

DOI: 10.4324/9781003254973-11

This view of law as infrastructural rather than super-structural underpins numerous studies in the critical socio-legal studies tradition. One contribution I have made to this literature is showing that the deeply intimate category of 'sexual orientation' was in fact generated from the 1970s onward by creative uses of existing legal categories and mechanisms, including analogizing sexual identity to 'race' as it existed in US law.[1] In Canada, where I had a short-term career as an expert witness on 'the sociology of sexuality' (despite not being a sociologist, but that's another story) sexual orientation did not have to be construed specifically as similar to the biologized 'race' of US law, but Canadian courts came to accept the claim, made by activists and their lawyers, that sexual orientation is sufficiently similar to the other prohibited grounds of discrimination as to justify 'reading in' (a curious legal term of art) sexual orientation into anti-discrimination statutes. That law can be changed without legislators stirring long enough to write a new text is, of course, a key feature of the common law, and the Supreme Court of Canada has long exercised its common-law power to pull political chestnuts out of the fire for legislatures by 'reading in' words that aren't in the relevant texts. But the key point is that in numerous jurisdictions around the world, formal law (whether in the form of human rights statutes or in other forms, such as innovative Supreme Court decisions) has been deployed to limit the reach of homophobic actions and even opinions. Law is here seen as acting from above on a social world in which harmful prejudices are seen as vanishing all too slowly, if at all. Of course, such laws and authoritative judicial decisions, acting 'from above', can promote social justice; I would never underestimate the need for human rights-oriented law reform. But my point here, by way of conclusion to this book, is that in this more recent, less mainstream view, law is not portrayed as above civil society but rather as an integral part of the glue or the cement or the social trust – different readers will prefer different metaphors – that has brought particular civil societies into being. My own research on the genealogy of 'sexual orientation' showed that North American activists invented the term for purposes of lawsuits and constitutional challenges, drawing on the previous success of gender and race anti-discrimination jurisprudence. Later on, say by the 1990s, 'sexual orientation' came to be used, especially by young people, to

---

1 Mariana Valverde, *Law's dream of a common knowledge* (Princeton, NJ, Princeton University Press, 2003), Chapters 4 and 5.

describe their own identities, but it was a term originally created to fight legal battles with law's own reasoning. The political project was to ban discrimination against gays and lesbians and bisexuals and trans people, but since liberal legal systems insist on theoretically neutral terms ('gender', not women, and 'race', not Black people), a term analogous to race and gender as they appear in law had to be devised to build a new category that potentially included everyone.

Socio-legal studies has in recent years seen a veritable outpouring of studies that one could categorize as forming an 'infra-turn'. In Australia, international law expert Fleur Johns has influentially argued that legal scholarship ought to focus more on what she calls "infralegalities".[2] One good example is Johns' own study of the infralegalities of the Guantanamo Bay prison; she shows that the usual lawyerly focus on prisoners' deprivation of legal rights prevents us from seeing that the environment is not a legal black hole, as it has often been portrayed; in fact, it is reconstituted every day through myriad legal rules and norms that govern in excruciating detail what the US military does at the military base including its prisoner camp.

Similarly, another international law scholar with much influence on socio-legal studies, Annelise Riles, has emphasized that focusing on the "technicalities" of law can be extremely productive. Her argument is that the so-called technicalities can matter more than the grand principles of democracy in shaping outcomes, in courtrooms and beyond.[3] This type of argument draws attention to processes that go on before the law or off to the side – such as deciding which set of rules will be used to adjudicate a particular matter for which either people or issues have gone across borders. Riles' focus is on legal 'technicalities', especially those utilized to adjudicate jurisdictional questions, but her argument is in sympathy with research by legal anthropologists showing that factors that are not strictly legal and that are not part of the official record – courtroom architecture, the choice of language, witnesses' demeanour and clothing – have important effects not only on

---

2 Fleur Johns, *Non-legality in international law: unruly law* (Cambridge, Cambridge University Press, 2013). See also Gavin Sullivan, *The law of the list: UN counterterrorism practices and the politics of international security* (Cambridge, Cambridge University Press, 2020). Sullivan borrows the term 'infra-legalities' from Johns.

3 Annelise Riles, "A new agenda for the cultural study of law: taking on the technicalities" *Buffalo Law Review*, vol. 53, 2005, 973–1034; Mariana Valverde, "Jurisdiction and scale: legal 'technicalities' as resources for theory" *Social and Legal Studies*, vol. 18, no. 2, 2009, 139–57.

some legal outcomes but also on the way in which 'law' is practiced and experienced. (These are not dissimilar to Fleur Johns' 'non-legalities'.) All legal anthropology is concerned with the 'infra' of law – the cultural assumptions, the human behaviours, and the arrangements of objects that seem 'natural' to the participants and are therefore largely invisible to the lawyerly gaze. But to this Riles adds a new twist, showing that it is in fact impossible to separate the 'infra' of law (in the sense of background cultural assumptions) from law's sinews and bones, the structures that organize legal processes and make them flow along certain channels and not others.

This book locates itself firmly on the side of 'infralegalities' and 'technicalities'. However, perhaps because I am not a law professor or even a plain lawyer, I focus a little more than Riles and Johns on processes, governing tools, and norms that are not strictly part of formal law but that in practice are intertwined with law. In a sense, then, I am not so much taking sides with the 'infra' but questioning the very notion that there is an above and a below, a superstructure of legal rules versus an everyday world of social norms.

For example, in Chapter 6, featuring the British HS2 rail project as a case study, I focus on the fact that this ambitious infrastructure project (insofar as it exists, which as of 2021 is not very far) has been put together by means of instances of the core private law tool known as a contract – instead of through public law, including planning law. But much attention is paid as well to the socio-economic particularities of the contracts – such as the fact that most of the big firms poised to benefit from HS2 contracts are based in EU countries, a blow to the government's optimistic rhetoric about the 'supply-chain' benefits of the project for post-Brexit Britain. The fact that the HS2 was initially conceived when the UK was still within the EU may well have been a key fact, a legal fact, but, simultaneously, the political economy of large European corporations operating in many countries is not a mere product of law, EU or any other law.

This example draws attention to a question that has haunted the field of socio-legal studies from the beginning – namely, should one even attempt to 'draw the line' separating 'law' from 'society' or from 'the economy'? Socio-legal studies were once (say in the 1950s and 1960s) focused on the social, largely structural preconditions of law – such as what the pioneering French sociologist Emil Durkheim famously called "the precontractual conditions of contract" (the social trust that needs to exist before contracts can become widely used). Early legal anthropology similarly drew attention to the large-scale culturally specific assumptions embedded in various legal systems (for instance, the linear teleological temporality associated with Judeo-Christian thought, which grounds good parts of Western law but stands in sharp contrast to non-Western temporalities). The aim of such studies was, to oversimplify, to document how 'society' influences both the architecture of legal systems and specific legal content.

By contrast, today's scholarship on 'law and society' tends to be wary of any and all attempts to delineate the boundary between the legal and the extra-legal or the pre-legal. For the purposes of a lawsuit or a prosecution, it is certainly important to draw a line separating legal factors from legally irrelevant factors. Borrowing a phrase from legal philosopher Peter Goodrich, we can say that law students (in England at any rate) have to be taught that the average man supposedly found riding the Clapham omnibus enjoys a reasoning power not affected by the vehicle's destination. An 'infra' approach, by contrast, might ask, Why does the textbook mention Clapham? Why not Wigan? Why not Windsor?

But by contrast with legal practice, where practitioners do have to divide 'facts' into legally relevant and legally irrelevant, many scholarly studies today draw attention to the unintended and often negative effects of trying to 'draw the line' around law. To say that Clapham matters to English lawyers' notions of common sense might be going too far, but to say that Clapham is irrelevant and could be substituted by any other locale would also be going too far. And the mode of transport, as indicated in Chapter 6, is also not exactly irrelevant. There are good reasons why neither a private airplane nor a luxury yacht would work for the legal cliché. Fleur Johns' investigations of various empirical-legal sites, cited earlier, document not only the constitutive effects of law on the social and the economic but also the way in which private norms as well as habits of seeing and governing that one might call 'cultural' are intertwined with law.

This new wariness about attempting to separate 'law' from 'non-law' is also found in studies within the rapidly growing 'legal geography' literature. For instance, Irus Braverman's influential study of the political and legal uses of different kinds of trees in Israel-Palestine is fruitful for socio-legal studies around the world precisely because it refuses to separate law from non-law.[4] In her account, the physical character of (Jewish) pine trees and (Palestinian) olive trees is treated

---

4 Irus Braverman, *Planted flags: trees, land and law in Israel/Palestine* (Cambridge, Cambridge University Press, 2009).

as relevant, alongside the cultural and economic meanings of these competing forms of vegetation. Her investigation shows how the Israeli occupation reproduces itself through law, through ideology, and through physical rearrangements of earth, vegetation, rocks, houses, and roads – simultaneously.

Even outside of socio-legal studies one can find studies that, in keeping with currently popular actor-network methodology, treat their object of study (say, cities) as a hybrid assemblage of laws, norms, concrete, bricks, vehicles, wires, and pipes, although such studies of urban life and infrastructure usually underplay or even ignore the role of laws and regulations in constituting the built environment.[5]

I thus hope that this book has not only provided readers some information that can be useful to promote citizen activism and civic participation but has also shown, through doing more than telling, that the machinery of law is integral to infrastructure planning and delivery, even if that is not obvious because infrastructure promoters prefer to show pretty pictures.

That is what socio-legal studies is about: showing the 'law' within the 'society' and also the 'society' within law, without imagining that the two dimensions are actually separate.

But at this point, I feel obliged to bring to a halt this concluding reflection. The reason for not wanting to prolong it, pleasurable as it is to write in generalities rather than in documented case studies, is that the argument in this concluding chapter risks falling victim to the perennial academic temptation of describing one's own work as the culmination of past trends, as uniquely timely because it simultaneously includes and supersedes previous scholarly traditions.[6]

While uncomfortably aware of the temptation to describe my own work as somehow the culmination of the workings of history, I would nevertheless like to make it explicit – as the substantive chapters show

---

5 A recent influential example of this literature is Ash Amin and Nigel Thrift, *Seeing like a city* (Cambridge, Polity, 2017).
6 The philosopher Hegel's influences are today usually unintended because few social scientists or lawyers study his rather impenetrable work. But the least worthwhile aspect of Hegel's thought – the Eurocentric arrogance that allowed him to see all previous philosophy as unwittingly culminating in his own spacetime and even in his own head – is unfortunately prevalent among theoretically inclined social scientists. By contrast, the Hegelian dialectic, arguably a less Eurocentric and masculinist form of reasoning, has fallen into complete disuse, perhaps because of the decline of Marxist thought, which was for much of the twentieth century the main site of dialectical analysis.

implicitly – that this book's concern with documenting practices found throughout the world of infrastructure planning and delivery is in keeping not only with much contemporary social theory (with its talk of assemblages, hybrid networks, and governing practices) but also with a certain stream within the only field I can call my own, socio-legal studies: the recent tradition that focuses attention on complex relationships quietly linking larger economic, social, and political power relations to the seldom studied workings of quasi-legal or infra-legal 'minor' governing practices.

The 'infra' of law is not quite an 'infrastructure' in the conventional sense, obviously. But if being aware of living in the Anthropocene means that we avoid setting human reason including legal reason above and beyond natural and other material relations, learning to see law as infrastructural rather than super-structural becomes an intellectual project that is larger than but exemplified by this little book's effort to understand the legal and governance underpinnings of material infrastructures.

Index

accountability 6–8, 20, 24–5, 87, 101, 113
Africa 5, 60
airline travel 71, 74
American New Deal (1930s) 3, 57, 66
anthropologists 62, 115
Argentina: debt crisis 48, 51–3
Arnstein, Sherry 37
audit: gender equality 18; methods 15, 17–18; safety audits 16; supply chain 15
auditor-general 25–7, 111
Audit Society, The: Rituals of Verification (Power) 15
Austen, Jane 28
Australia 6, 87, 115
Australian 7, 111

Bachelet, Nichelle (Chile) 106
bankruptcy 31, 47, 50, 54
Baptista, Idalina 60–1
Barcelona, Spain 72, 97
Berkely, Tony 64, 74
Bhubaneswar, India 100–2
Biden, Joseph 14, 66, 68
Big Brother 97–8
bonds: Argentinian 51, 53; emerging market bonds 52; government 28–9, 31, 51, 85; municipal 34, 100; revenue 31–2; treasury 30; war bonds 28–31
Braverman, Irus 117
Brazil 89, 98
Britain 34, 59, 64, 70, 74, 76, 116

British: consol 28–9, 85; government bonds 28; Green Book 107; high speed rail 13, 59–60, 63, 65, 116
British Columbia, Canada 83, 105
British Department of Transport: Strength in Numbers 112
British Private Finance Initiative 83
Buenos Aires 52, 70
build back better 63–4, 69

California 68
Canada: auditor-general 26; co-management 37; Post Office closures 9
carbon emissions 65
Carney, Mark 19
Chile 105–7
Cisco (technology company) 93, 99, 102
Citizenship and Infrastructure (Lemanski) 5
Clinton, Bill 68
closed-circuit television (CCTV) 94–5, 101
collateral 46
conflict-of-interest 49
construction 5, 11, 55, 76, 86, 104, 109; *see also* infrastructure
consultation: community 13, 36–8, 40, 43; public 36–7, 41–2, 79–80
consumer 15, 20, 84
contract: bidding for 76, 82; clauses 57, 85, 100, 109; government by 87; infrastructure 85–6; law 116; planning by 7, 87; for services 79, 81

contractor 38, 82
corporation: audit 18; databases 79;
    municipal 33; private, for profit
    67, 95
costs 40, 76, 93, 105–6, 109, 112
COVID-19: inquests into 26; recovery
    funds 14; supply-chain myths 75;
    travel restrictions 63, 69, 73
credit cards 52
Credit Karma 45
credit ratings: agency/agencies 45,
    48–9, 53; governmental 45–6, 85,
    102, 110; individual/personal 45–6;
    scores 45–6, 48–9
credit risk(s) 47

Daniels (developer) 80
Dannin, Ellen 87
Datta, Ayona 102
deals 9, 21, 54–7, 65; see also
    infrastructure
Delhi, India 97, 106
Deloitte (consulting firm) 20, 111
democracy 1, 13, 20, 83, 111
Durkheim, Emil 116

electricity 8, 46, 59–61, 90, 92
Enron 50
Equifax 45, 48
Ernst and Young (consulting firm) 111
Espeland, Wendy 16, 112
Eurostar 60

financial: advisor 48; autonomy
    (municipal) 102; behavior 46;
    bias 50; crisis 48, 50; health 102;
    regulators 50; resources 33; risks 19;
    security 28–9; statement 16, 53
Flynn, Alexandria 79
Forster, Edward Morgan 28
Foucault, Michel 1, 25
France 74
Freedman, Mark 87
Freeman, Jo 87
French: engineering 75; railway
    system 4, 60, 68, 73–4

global North: credit ratings, perks
    30; governments 2, 9, 12, 53;

infrastructure planning 9–10, 21,
    60, 94
global South: governments 12, 23,
    77–8; infrastructure planning 36,
    53, 59–61; procurement practices 2,
    7, 9–10, 22
Goldman Sachs 53
Google 39, 79, 98
government: credit ratings 45–6, 49;
    revenues 47
Graham, Steven 5, 60
Green Book (British) 107
green spaces 67
Guantanamo Bay 115

Harvard University 51
high-speed rail: California's planned
    68; eco-friendly transportation
    63; long-term project/expense 60,
    63–4; myth of 64, 67
Hitachi (Japan) 99, 102
Ho, Karen 51
Hodge, Gerald 6
Hodge, Graeme 87
housing authority 80
Howards End (Forester) 28
HS2: dissenting reports 64, 74;
    funding 75–6; high-speed train
    project 13, 60, 63–5, 77; jobs report
    76

IBM (International Business
    Machines) Corporation 79, 93, 99,
    102
IMF (international monetary fund)
    9–10, 24, 46, 51–2
India 60, 68, 95, 100, 103
Indian government (India) 100, 102
inflation 29, 52–3, 84
information technology (IT)
    (managers/specialists) 95, 97, 99,
    103
infrastructure: alternative approaches
    60; best infrastructures 60;
    construction 67, 69; consultations
    36–7; contracts 85–6; deals 61,
    81–2, 98; financing 85; increased
    taxes 1, 47, 53; innovation in 94,
    105, 109; investing in 85;

large-scale 67, 76; long-term projects 86; new deal-style 66; planning, democratic 62; as railway building 3–4; re-nationalizing 88; top-down projects 3, 36, 59, 89
infrastructure projects: environmental concerns 7, 15, 36–7, 43–4, 63; evaluations systems 22–3; not subject to audit 17, 23; welfare state 3
Infrastructure, Ontario (Canada) 68, 83, 85, 105, 111
innovation 73, 89, 93–4, 100, 105, 109
inquiry 1, 19, 25–6
interest rates 30, 46
International Handbook of Public- Private Partnerships (Hodge et al) 86
iPhone 45
Ivy League 50

Jacobs, Jane 57, 93
Japan 30, 68
Johns, Fleur 115–17
Johnson, Boris 76–7, 107
Journal of Economic Perspectives 49
jurisdictions 8, 11, 74, 95, 99, 105

Kitchin, Rob 96
KPMG (British/Dutch consulting company) 20, 111

Ladder of Citizen Participation, A (Arnstein) 37
law: administrative (scholars) 6, 87, 113; business 79; common 36, 89, 114; contract 116; corporate 83, 87; criminal 113; international 7, 115; mainstream media thoughts on 113; private 6–7, 87, 89, 110, 116; public 6, 8, 89, 116; US Law 16, 47, 114
left-wing 3, 8, 19, 67, 88
legal: rules (national) 37, 115–6; studies (socio-legal) 6, 114–19
legal consent 48
Lehman Brothers 50
lending 29, 40, 84
liberal 2, 40, 115
Liberty Bond 30
loans 48–9, 89
London School of Economics (LSE) 15

London-Birmingham-Crewe line 77
low income 41, 48, 70, 101
Luque-Ayala, Andrés 97

marketing: campaigns 28, 39, 70, 95; image-reliant 11, 67
Marvin, Simon 5–6, 60, 97
McFarlane, Colin 60
McKinsey (consulting firm) 20, 102
Mekong River 7
Metrolinx 40
Metropolitan Board of Works, London 3
Mexico City subway disaster 55
Modi, Narendra (India) 95, 100, 102
money: borrowed 34–5, 43, 46, 48, 110; flow of 15, 60; government spending of 29, 31–2, 77; public 14, 42, 77; value for money 17, 104
Montreal, Canada 58, 70, 109
Moody's 50
Moore, Aaron 80
mortgage holders 48
mortgage(s) 30, 48, 84
Mozambique, South Africa 60

negotiations (behind-the-scenes) 11
neoliberal: era 98, 106; government 3, 23, 32; views 3, 22, 60
New Jersey 33, 54
New York City, New York 46, 49–50, 54, 97, 102
New York Times 55
NIMBY (not-in-my-back-yard) Conservatives 74
non-governmental organizations (NGO's) 18, 78
North America 48, 94

Ontario, Canada 12, 26, 80, 110
Operations Evaluation Department: The First 30 Years (World Bank website) 22
Organization for Economic Co-operation and Development (OECD) 105

Parliament 75
partnership 37, 78–81, 87

Partnerships BC (Canada) 68, 83, 105, 111
pension funds 85; as finance capital 42, 83–5
Peron, Juan (Eva) 51
Piketty, Thomas 29
policymakers 10, 62
politicians: opposition 20, 26, 32, 64; political gain maneuvering 55–6
Port Authority of New York 33–4, 102
Power, Michael 15, 18
premium spaces 6, 6 2, 60
Pride and Prejudice 28
Princeton University 50
Private Finance Initiative (PFI) 83, 105, 107–8, 111
private law 6–7, 87, 89, 110, 116
proposals 89, 97, 100, 102
public: authority 82–3, 88, 108; infrastructure 65, 85; works 1, 3, 9, 13, 68, 84, 87, 105, 109
public law 6, 8, 89, 116
public lawyers 6–7, 87
public sector: boondoggles 12, 109; pension funds 84–5; unions 9, 106; workers 9
public transit 39, 81, 88, 95
public-private partnerships (PPPs) 1–4, 20, 79, 88, 98, 108
Public-Sector Comparator (PSC) 106–7, 110

rail: high-speed (*see* high-speed rail); passenger 68–9
Reagan, Ronald 49, 65
reliable 2, 49, 59
renege (on debt) 47
right-wing 2–3, 19–20
rights: human 112, 114; social/economic 90
Riles, Annelise 115–16
Rio de Janeiro, Brazil 97
Rio Olympics 98
Roosevelt, Franklin D. (FDR) 3, 34
Roy, Ananya 60
rule of law 1

Scotland 73, 75
Scott, James 58

Securities and Exchange Commission, New York 49
Seeing Like a State (Scott) 57–8
Siemens (innovative technology company) 93, 99
sexual orientation 114
Sidewalk Labs 38, 79
Sidewalk Toronto 80
smart cities: data collections/databases 91–2; pursuit of smartness 91–2; technology dependent solution 79, 90–4
smart street light 93, 96
SNCF, France 68, 73
socio-legal: literature 5–6; studies 6–7, 115–18
sovereignty 47, 51, 83
Spain 52, 68, 71–4
special purpose vehicle (SPV) 102
Splintering Urbanism (Marvin) 6
stocks and bonds 85
subway 40, 55
supply chain benefits 75–6, 116
surveillance capitalism 92
sustainable 2, 62

TALGO 73
TGV's (Train à Grande Vitesse, "high-speed train") French 60, 73
Thatcher, Margaret (government of) 8, 64–5, 86
top-down 68; *see also* infrastructure
Toronto Community Housing Company 80
Toronto, Canada 40–1, 52, 58, 99–100
tourism 63, 72
train: freight 74; passenger 70, 74
transparency 18–20, 25, 49, 102, 113
Transparency International 12
TransUnion 45, 48
travel time 65
Trump, Donald J. 1, 47–8, 54
Trump: The Art of the Deal (Trump) 54
truth 1, 12, 45–6

United Kingdom (UK) 30, 58, 63, 107, 116
United Nations (UN) 17, 23–4, 90

Urban Operating Systems: Producing the Computational City &Luque-Ayala/ Marvin) 97
urban studies 5, 11, 61, 66
Urban Studies (journal) 61

value for money (VFM): calculation and justification means 105, 108, 110
visible/visibility 25, 111

Wales 75
Wall Street (film) 54

Wall Street, New York 46, 51
welfare state 2–3, 25, 58, 68
White House, Washington D.C. 47, 54
World Bank: infrastructure evaluation system 22–4; workshop on VFM 105–8
World Cup (football) 98
World War I 29, 71
World War II 2, 25, 30, 51, 58, 71

Yale University 50